Deer Dad

A Hunter's Guide

By
Michael M. Warren
in collaboration with Buck the Deer

To
Bartell and Jim Zachry
my hosts
and
Al Brothers
my mentor

Contents and Synopsis

Introduction

Deer Reader:

I thought I'd write a brief note about this book. I suppose one might be a bit confused about all of this. I mean, where does a deer get off writing a book in the first place? For that matter, where does a deer get off just plain writing? Everyone knows deer can't write—right? Even if they could hold a pen, it does require a certain intelligence and higher reasoning power to put words on paper in a meaningful way. So, this whole thing may seem absurd.

On the other hand, those of you that are serious hunters will immediately recognize that deer are quite intelligent indeed. We can easily master the rather simple techniques of thinking and writing. Remember that buck that you have been catching glimpses of for years, the one that you know is out there, that you sometimes hear laughing at you from behind a tree? If I'm smart enough to elude you all this time, I certainly am smart enough to communicate in such a rudimentary fashion as writing a letter. I mean, I'm not trying to call you on the phone, (although I think I could if I really wanted to, but to tell you the truth the buttons are just too close together for me to press accurately).

Anyway, what's the point in all of this? I can write, I do write, and I will write for many years to come. Most often, I have written to my father. In fact, through the years he has accumulated a large number of letters I have written to him. He recently came to visit me and brought them with him to reminisce. He is getting a bit old, and reliving old times makes him happy. As we were looking through the letters, and even as I was writing them, thoughts occurred to both of us that humans might like to share the messages. I will admit that some of them are rather personal. Also, some of them contain some rather important survival information that has allowed me to mature and reach my prime years. I know there is a risk publishing this material and that my own future and the future of many of my close relatives is at stake, but as I consider the risks, the past performance of humans in hunting practices is such that I feel the risk is rather small. Besides, my publisher informs me that thousands of humans will be paying for this book and that I will receive a handsome share in the profits. Since there are some investments I want to make for my old age, I could certainly use the income.

What follows, therefore, is a compilation of letters I have written to my father. In retrospect, some of them are quite interesting and educational. In fact, if you humans study these letters carefully and follow the advice I give, you will undoubtedly improve your hunting and game management techniques. Actually that will help both deer and humans. Some of the letters are funny, some sad, some good, and some bad (remember I'm not a poet). I hope you will enjoy them.

Please, remember that although these letters contain much useful information about hunting and game management techniques, they are not meant to be a complete information source. To provide complete information would require several large volumes and even then the information would be obsolete even before the books were published. Research in hunting techniques and game management is constantly developing and the intelligent hunter must utilize several sources to continuously educate himself.

By the way, I am a whitetail deer, and I live in the southern part of Texas. I represent a noble species. My cousins and I grow to quite large sizes and are able to develop trophy quality and even record breaking racks if conditions are right. I recognize that, depending on where you live, whitetail deer may or may not be available. However, my species stretches from the eastern coast of the United States to the western plains and from Mexico to Canada. The mule deer and the black tail deer are our western relatives and, believe me, they are nothing to sneeze at; however, since I know myself and my close relatives best, most of my remarks will be made about us, and much of the geography will be about south Texas, a beautiful part of the country to which I invite all of you (without your rifles).

Sincerely,

Buck

Prodigal Son Returns

Deer Dad:

I hope this letter finds you well. I know it's been a long time since you've heard from me. Several years, in fact, have passed since I left home. Much water has gone over the dam in that time and I have come to realize that my roots are indeed important to me. I hope you will forgive me for leaving when I did. Obviously, I had to get away and do my own thing. I do remember you telling me that you did the same thing when you were that age, so I guess it's just in the genes.

Well, I want to bring you up to date on what has happened to me, and I also want to keep in touch from now on so that we can continue the wonderful relationship we had before I left home.

I have found a perfect place to live. I have a fine ranch here in south Texas near Laredo. I have good food and water available and I have grown quite large and each season sport a fine set of antlers which have actually become something of a conversation piece among deer and hunters alike.

Speaking about hunters, I also have a fine set of hunters who come around each season and try to find me. When I say a fine set of hunters, I actually mean a rather poor set of hunters. Not in the monetary sense (I have never seen a financially poor hunter— hunting is not a poor man's sport), but they are poor in the hunting ability sense. That is good for me. I have learned a great deal about the correct way to hunt and also about how my hunters hunt. Fortunately, both techniques are not the same. Could I give them lessons? Maybe someday I will.

Anyway, I like my home, I like my hunters, and I really like my landowner. The human that owns this property is interested in developing the deer in order to produce a high quality herd. This is to our advantage. He has taken the necessary steps to succeed. I will tell you about him in future letters.

That's enough about me; how about you? I really do want to hear from you. I am worried that your health may be slipping. I have already found there are some things I could do as a young buck that are becoming more and more difficult for me now. I hope you are holding up against all the pressures of the hunters and the land developers, and you are not having to face hunting season and condominium builders as well. It gets harder and harder to move to a new home as you get older. If it's necessary, you could come down here and live near me. I am secure enough now that we could be neighbors. I'd just have to figure a way to get you past the high fence we have around the property. I'm sure we could work it out.

Let me tell you this. Since I really do miss you, I intend to write you often to let you know what is happening to me. If you want to, you can keep the letters and collect the series. Who knows? Someday they may make a great book that we can share with the world. We'll just have to figure out which world we want to share them with—the deer world or the human world. Maybe we should do both.

I have to go now. It's dark here and the landowner has planted a very nice oat field for us near his house. I think I'll go up there and have some for dessert.

I'll write again soon.

Love,

Buck

Cave Man

Deer Dad:

The weather is warm and sunny today. The visibility is quite clear, so I thought I would hide in some thick brush and write you a letter. Actually, I have been doing some interesting research into our history and I thought I would tell you a bit about what I found. The family library really has some interesting books. I decided to decipher some of the earliest books in the collection. You know, the ones written on scrolls in that ancient language. Well, I have managed to translate some of them.

Would you believe that our ancestors had many of the same problems that we have today? I think there have always been hunters around to worry about. Of course, our biggest enemy is the dreaded HOMO SAPIENS, the human. In the earliest times, before humans existed, when their ancestors were fish swimming about we still had plenty of worries. There were wild carnivores who would stalk our ancestors and prey on them. As now, our ancient relatives ate nothing but plants, shrubs, and the like, but many other large animals actually ate us and other animals like us.

Once the human beings did come along, things got a good deal worse. They liked to hunt us not only because of our tasty meat but also for our warm hides, our bones which could be made into tools, and for many other uses they figured out during the long winters they spent in their caves.

Oh! That's right!. They lived in caves. They were called "cave men." I suppose some of them were called "cave women." They finally discovered fire, how to make clothing, and, then, worst of all, how to make tools and weapons. The weapons weren't much, just some clubs and spears, but cave men got quite sophisticated in weapon construction and even more clever in finding uses. None of our ancestors were safe when these humans got together and formed hunting parties.

Of course, our ancestors were far from wiped out. They did have some defenses. They could see the cave men, smell them, and hear them—just as we can. Humans weren't as easy to smell then as they are today. Since they never bathed, they usually smelled like whatever they were around last. Today, of course, hunters usually smell like "Dial" or "Lifebuoy"; then they go and cover up their scent with manufactured imitation animal scent that is supposed to fool us. You know all about that.

Anyway, since these ancient humans really needed us for their survival, hunted us only when necessary, and used virtually all of us when they did catch us, I guess it wasn't too bad. I did not read anywhere that any of these "cave men" had our heads mounted to hang in their caves for display purposes as humans do today.

Well, Dad, it's getting dark, and I think I'll go get something to eat. This history stuff is pretty interesting. I think I'll study it some more and write you again with periodic updates.

Take care of yourself.

Love,

Buck

Wheels

Deer Dad:

I hope this letter finds you well. I was looking through our history books again. It really is interesting and educational. I forget which of our uncles said it, but I am convinced if we "don't understand our history we are bound to repeat its mistakes."

There certainly have been a great many important contributions to our development through the ages. I'm proud of the way our species has adapted to our environment and modified our behavior in order to survive.

One of our biggest survival tests has been human beings. They have developed many ingenious methods calculated to hasten our destruction. Weapons have been a good example of this effort, but I will have to leave that to another letter. The single most important tactic they have perfected is the horse. What I mean is, their single-minded strategy has become to utilize transportation to try to neutralize our speed and ability to run away from danger.

The thing is they had this tactic and then they went and lost it. I learned from my research that many centuries ago humans found a way to tame (they call it domesticate) the horse and harness this lovely animal for their own needs. Horses have been used to carry humans, haul cargo, pull wagons, tote sleds, run in races, and even dance in shows. At one point, an enterprising human figured out that a horse could run after a deer and, even though he couldn't catch one, could bring the human close enough to use a weapon to kill successfully. Then it was "Katie bar the door." There were horses everywhere with hunters chasing all kinds of game from deer to foxes. Yes, Dad, little red and brown foxes were chased by big horses, dogs, and hunters dressed in funny red suits with little black hats blowing tin horns and shouting "yoikes," (whatever that means).

Horses were tough to compete with. They could run in any direction at varying speeds to match a deer for short distances, so if you were not on your toes and were caught napping you could be

7

in real trouble. The only good part was that while horses were good, the riders were usually not. They were afraid to go fast and often fell off the horse during a chase or got tired and quit too soon. Still, horses were not too good for us.

Where humans made their mistake was that they got too fancy for horses. Somehow, the horse was replaced by another mode of transportation that humans call a "pickup truck." Legs were replaced by wheels, a heart by a motor, and a brain by something they call a transmission. Instead of riding on top of the horse, where humans could see well, they decided to sit inside the contraption where visibility became severely limited and mobility even more. I can't tell you the number of times I have watched these humans spot a deer from inside a pickup truck and then go through all sorts of maneuvers to try to get out of the truck to get a shot, or even sillier, to try to shoot from inside the truck. Crazy!

The horse could go anywhere, through almost any kind of country with ease. The pickup truck has to go on roads because of its wheels' limited function. Humans must think if they build a road somewhere we deer will surely be attracted to the road and hunters will have an easy time finding and shooting us. Do you believe it?

I hope they never go back to the horse and leave the pickup truck. It's very comforting to be able to hear the truck motor from several miles away so that we can take evasive action earlier. It is disappointing that so many of our species can't seem to get it into their heads that trucks are bad. Still, to be minding your own business and have a horse and "expert" hunter sneak up on you is even more disquieting.

I think I'll end now. I know you have trouble reading long letters because your eyes get tired. Oh, by the way, I read in a human book that eating carrots is good for your eyes. Why don't you sneak into the vegetable garden tonight? Humans eat carrots and can't see well, but it couldn't hurt to try. Let me know if it works. I'll write again soon. I want to tell you about some other animals and how humans have trained them to help hunt.

Love,

Buck

Hounds

Deer Dad:

I told you I would write again about other animals used by the humans to help them hunt us. Fortunately, humans have a great deal of trouble once they set out to hunt deer. While their ancient ancestors were good hunters, modern humans have lost most of the abilities that were acquired with such difficulty by their forebears. Most humans live in big cities all year round, then expect to come to the country for a weekend and go home with a trophy suitable for mounting on a wall. Their ability to track, recognize, stalk, and shoot is minimal at best. What they really need is all the help they can get. That's why they learned to use horses and pickup trucks to help them.

One of the hardest jobs they have is locating deer. I already told you their eyesight is poor. Their sense of smell is even worse, and their hearing won't help them much if we stay quiet.

They did do one clever thing to locate deer. They trained other animals to help. I already told you about the horse. Now I want to remind you about the dog. I use the term "remind" because I know you are already aware about using dogs to locate deer, even though you didn't know about the human's use of horses. Even today some hunters use dogs, although in many places it is illegal. I have had some considerable experience with hunters committing illegal activities. I will write you about them sometime.

Dogs are clever animals. They are easily trained to do many things. They fetch very well. Humans have them fetching all sorts of things. For example, they fetch slippers, newspapers, balls, ducks, and sticks. They watch very well. Humans have them watching many things also. For example, they watch houses, prisons, airports, and office buildings. They also find very well. Humans also have them find many things. They find drugs, escaped convicts, buried bones, and other treasure, and they also find game, especially foxes (see wheels) birds, coons, and deer.

The dogs do this by scent. They have a very keen sense of smell. So do we, but the difference is dogs are easily domesticated and can live around the house. It's not as easy to domesticate a deer to the point of being house broken. Not only that, but our horns get in the way. Most apartment owners won't allow dogs as pets, much less deer.

Anyway, the dogs can be trained to hunt well. They also like hunting because they get rewards for success. I think one day I may get a dog to train. Think of all the good uses I would have for a well trained dog.

So, the dogs find us and then set up a racket to tell the hunters where we are. There aren't too many ways we can get away from them either. We can try to cross a large body of water and hope they lose the scent, but there aren't too many large bodies of water around. Besides, the dogs can swim well. We can try to find a place the dogs can't penetrate, but those little rascals can get just about anywhere. Of course, the hunters can't get into those very small places so we do have a chance to remain hidden from them. The other thing we can do is lead the dogs to a local game warden and let him catch the dogs and hunters using illegal tactics against us. This is a little known ploy that can be very successful. I always try to keep track of my local game warden at all times. I think I'll write a separate letter about him.

Please, Dad, watch out for dogs. There is a modification of the dog that some hunters use to find deer when they realize how inadequate their own senses are. Some enterprising hunters use machines known as helicopters to find deer. These infernal machines actually fly. Oh, they don't fly like regular airplanes, very fast and high. No, these machines fly low and slow, and I have even known them to stop in mid-air, believe it or not, for hunters to look for game. Our only advantage is that it is rather difficult to shoot from them with any accuracy. If we run a zig-zag pattern most hunters will find it hard to hit us. Looking from a helicopter is legal. Taking a census from a helicopter is legal, but hunting from one is illegal. Remember the friendly game warden. He can usually spot one of these machines flying around, especially during hunting season.

Well, that's enough for now. Take care of yourself. I'll write again soon.

Love,

Buck

Who's a Hunter

Deer Dad:

Humans are strange people. Hunters are even stranger. I have seen many hunters in my day. As you know, they come in all shapes and sizes. They are all ages, races, and even sexes. That's right, even some women hunt. I will admit not anywhere near the numbers of women hunt as their male counterparts, but some women are quite experienced and talented when it comes to the finer points of the art. Coming from a deer, that's quite a compliment. Women usually have a different attitude about the sport.

First of all, they pay attention to what they are doing. Men seem to get distracted very easily; their minds clearly wander. They think about all sorts of extraneous things like beer, booze, and babes. I'm not going to tell you that women don't think about men. I know better; they do, however, realize that if they are hunting it should be their first priority so they do give it their full attention. Remember there are still only a few women hunters and I suppose those that do participate are more highly motivated than men.

Let's get back to the men. Who are they? Most of them have plenty of money. I can tell that because of the way most of them spend it. They buy all sorts of fancy equipment and extraneous paraphernalia—expensive rifles, high priced clothes, scopes, and other stuff that I will tell you about in other letters.

Most of the hunters are city folk who hunt a few weekends a year and consider themselves experts from this meager experience. Yet they find it very difficult to accept advice from others, even from experts. They haven't got the time or inclination to do their own homework or fieldwork. They don't scout the terrain. They usually don't even bother to sight in their rifle before they get to camp.

Hunting takes preparation, concentration, and commitment. Most hunters neither realize nor practice these concepts. It's a wonder that they are successful at all. As it turns out, occasional

11

success serves to reinforce their bad habits, and they never progress past the neophyte stage.

There are many fine, even expert, hunters and game management authorities who have mightily tried to teach the proper precepts of hunting and game management. They enjoy only partial success. Many human books have been written about the proper hunting techniques. Ranchers and property owners, in general, have failed to realize the potential cash crop we deer represent. Those that do realize they can significantly benefit from studying the material already prepared for their use.

A concept as simple and straightforward as the correct buck to doe ratio is often totally ignored by property owners. In many instances the final words a dying rancher passes on to his descendents do not concern the disposition of his estate or some fatherly advice learned after many years of survival in the world. Rather, his last gasp is, "Don't let them shoot the does." When this is the basic philosophy of game management, it's very difficult to develop the kind of herd that produces pride.

I started off talking about hunters, and I ended up with ranchers and property owners. That's a whole letter in itself, and I will write about it again. Meanwhile, I hope you are being careful. Remember that there are so-called hunters that don't seem to worry about hunting season, private property, or any other regulations that our friends the game wardens and state Parks and Wildlife Departments have established for our protection. Please move only after dark and stay in safe territory. Remember you're not as agile as you once were.

Love,

Buck

Where to Hunt—Sutton's Law

Deer Dad:

The more I learn about humans the more I don't understand them. That's especially true about hunting. There are apparently many reasons why humans hunt deer. It's not as you think, Dad, that the only reason is to stock the larder for the winter. That may have been the reason many years ago for such hunters as the old pioneers like Davy Crockett, Daniel Boone, and Ronald Reagan, but today there are many other reasons.

Some hunt so they aren't hunted. That's right; they want to get away from their everyday world and from all their troubles and cares. They want to just get out into the country and avoid telephones, televisions, and something called ulcers. Others are looking for trophy deer suitable for mounting on their walls at home. Then they can tell tall tales about their successes. Some like to shoot rifles and don't care much what they shoot at as long as they make a lot of noise and kill some living thing. Often those types of people kill other people. Then there are a few that understand game management, survival of the fittest, and are truly interested in the scientific and naturalistic aspects of the sport.

No matter what their reasons, one of the most important questions they all have to face is where to hunt. That is an interesting question that has both simple and very complex aspects; it is not a question to be answered lightly.

First and foremost in answering this question is applying Sutton's Law. In case you aren't familiar with Sutton's Law, I will tell you what it says.

Willie Sutton was a Yankee (that tells you a lot about him already) from New York. He was well known in those parts because of his profession, which was robbing banks. Actually, he was a lousy bank robber. He always got caught. What he was very good at was escaping from jail. In that he was an expert. Nevertheless, as soon as he escaped he turned right around and robbed another bank.

One day, while facing the local judge after having been caught again, the judge asked him, "Willie, why do you keep robbing banks?" Willie looked the judge straight in the eye and with all candor replied, "But Judge, that's where the money is!" Sutton's Law says "GO WHERE THE MONEY IS."

In other words, the best place to hunt deer is where there are deer. Straight forward, you say? Not so simple. How does the hunter know where the deer are? Does he listen to his friends? Sometimes that's like telling where their secret fishing holes are located. Should he listen to so-called experts? Even humans know about experts. Should he read books? Books have the ring of authority, but are often only the author's opinion.

I'm not talking about where the whitetail deer are found in this country. The range of our family is actually quite wide. Whitetail are found from the east coast of the United States to the west coast (Oregon and Montana) and from Mexico to Canada. Within that range, however, the number and quality of the deer vary greatly. In fact, the number and quality of the deer vary greatly within much smaller geographical areas. It becomes essential, therefore, to identify the best places to hunt not only state by state, and county by county, but even acre by acre. Added to that is the problem that just about everyone is ahead of the novice by the time he starts to look. So, Dad, you can see how difficult the selection of a hunting site becomes.

Well, it turns out there are some good ways to find out where the deer are. Of course, it takes work, some research, and some actually getting out and checking the territory. Finding the deer is such an important point that I think I'll describe several types of hunting situations in my next several letters.

Meanwhile, Dad, take care of yourself, and may your home never be discovered.

Love,

Buck

Let's Go Public

Deer Dad:

Things have changed since you were young, Dad. Humans are finding it harder and harder to find places to hunt. Most landowners have discovered that the game naturally found on their land is indeed a valuable cash crop, sometimes even more valuable than beef. Hunting of all species has therefore assumed greater economic importance, and smart landowners will manage game as closely as they manage their other crops.

In the old days a hunter could just walk up to a landowner, even a total stranger, ask permission to hunt on the property, and usually get immediate verbal approval. Of course, the hunter had better have been smart enough to respect the property and its contents so that he could get approval the next time, guaranteeing that the landowner would not feel the need to chastise the hunter for any inappropriate activities.

Well, hunters can't get easy access anymore. Most every landowner is now interested in leasing hunting rights to hunters. Even though the landowner may not practice sound game management, he still wants to earn income from the game and will not give it away to a total stranger. That's not to say that every landowner will lease hunting rights; in fact, some of the best hunting properties remain closed to everyone except the property owners and their guests. No one is going to give hunting rights away anymore.

I will write you more about hunting on private property later. I do want to tell you my feelings about hunting on public land in this letter.

There are two types of hunting experiences available on public property. One is hunting directly under the control of the Parks and Wildlife Departments of the various states, usually in specially designated areas that belong to the departments. Hunting there is similar to hunting on private property, only often better, since the game management practices are usually good and the deer are of high quality.

That's not what I am calling public hunting. What I'm calling public is hunting on public lands without restrictions as to number, types, or practices of hunters. Most of this type of hunting occurs in the North (I guess you could call it Yankee hunting). Under these circumstances, once the hunter obtains a license, he can go anywhere (on public property) to hunt during the season. Public hunting is like war. It sounds like war, with barrage after barrage of gunfire aimed at anything that moves. It smells like war, with the odor of gunpowder everywhere, and it often looks like war with wounded and killed humans lying about in total disarray.

Smart hunters will try to find the least populated areas to hunt. They will wear all sorts of highly visible clothing, mostly with bright orange coloring. They will practice and preach gun and general outdoor safety. They will still be scared as hell, constantly looking over their shoulder to see who's behind them, and I don't mean a deer.

Often hunting injuries in these circumstances are accidental. Another hunter thought the moving bush was a deer not a hunter. Occasionally the fatalities are intentional. Hunters actually shoot each other over the ownership of a deer. Barbaric, you say? Right you are, but remember they are humans.

If all this is true, then why hunt on public land at all? That's simple. Public hunting may be the only way a human has to hunt. If it is, then humans will return year after year. I suppose some risk bodily injury for the thrill of the hunt, animal or human.

There really is a deep-seated hunting instinct in human beings. It must go all the way back to their caveman ancestors. I think it's present in all varieties of human cultures. There are some humans, however, who claim they would never even consider hunting as an activity, but other humans say nonhunters feel this way because they have never experienced hunting. Take the most urbanized individual, strip away a few layers of city sophistication, give him a taste of high quality hunting, and the result is a committed hunter infected with the worst disease of all—"hunteritis."

If hunting on public land is the only way a hunter has to participate, then he will hunt on public land. It's that simple. So is the hunter who only hunts this way, because with a little planning and money, he could usually do better.

That's about all for now. I will write later about other places and ways to hunt. Take care of yourself.

Love,

Buck

Public is too Public

Deer Dad:

After my last letter I think you got the impression that humans would much prefer to avoid the logistical problems and social stigma associated with hunting on public lands. That's right, they would. Their only other alternative, unless they are lucky enough to arrange a hunt on some wildlife-managed public land, is to hunt on private property.

There are several ways to do this. It can be a complicated business and, although I will describe the details to you, it may take a few letters to cover all the possibilities.

The simplest and by far the best method is for the hunter to actually own the property on which he wants to hunt. That way he is the landowner, and he makes the rules. He can decide when he hunts, where he hunts, and with whom he hunts.

Of course, he could go out and actually purchase the property. In most cases, that takes a great deal of money. I have been watching the process of land purchase for several years. What I hear most humans say is, "Look how expensive that ranch is now. Why, I remember when it only cost half as much. I should have bought it then. I can't afford it now."

Now, Dad, that confuses me a bit. Why didn't they buy it back then when it was half the price? I'll bet the hunter had only half as much money then and it still was too expensive. The point is good property will always seem too expensive to the buyer. It's strange to me but that same property is always too cheap to the seller. Humans are funny creatures. I don't think buying the property is really the best way to hunt for most humans. I guess as a last resort it will do, but there are better methods of avoiding public hunting.

Being born into a family that already owns property is good. That's a pretty painless method of owning land on which to hunt—eventually. The problem with being born into a family with property is that the human has to wait until he grows up to actually own the property. Until then, he has to put up with adults who will try to teach him about owning land and hunting as well as reading, writing, and other trivial matters. He will have to suffer through childhood and, worse, through adolescence and teenagehood until the adult (usually his father) will realize that the son does know what he is talking about. Then maybe the son will come to own the land and make his own rules.

It does take a long time if the hunter intends to use the system of being born into the family with the land. Also, there is a certain amount of luck involved in picking the right family. If he is not careful he may end up in some place like New York City, where the only deer he will see is in a school book or perhaps in the form of gloves on some ladies' hands.

The other tried and true method of actually owning the land on which he will hunt is for the hunter to marry someone who already owns the land. That's the quickest method. I will admit it has a few drawbacks, but he will just have to weigh the advantages of acquiring the land to the disadvantages of marriage.

Dad, I suppose I ought to tell you just a few of the disadvantages of what humans call marriage. First of all, hunting season is only a few months long. Marriage lasts twelve months every year. It's no problem to escape to his deer blind during the season, but the hunter better have a really good story to explain the necessity of getting out there in June or July. His wife may think he is trying to avoid her.

Another disadvantage is that his wife may have parents, brothers, and sisters, all of whom think they may also have some claim to hunt on the property. These other people (humans call them inlaws) may go about making it difficult for him to run the place his way and hunt as he sees fit. They may have their own ideas that conflict with his.

Worse than that, his wife may have her own ideas about what she wants him to do during hunting season, such as going to the city to shop or attend the theater or other cultural events, visiting relatives (hers), leaving the country (USA), or any of a million other activities that directly conflict with his priorities.

I know to you, Dad, these conflicts seem trivial. The concept of marriage or monogamy is not quite sophisticated enough to bother a deer. We have a much better social structure; but to a human this can be a real problem, with precious few solutions. The human doesn't want to divorce his wife. The property will go with her. He certainly doesn't want to miss hunting by agreeing to participate in these other superfluous activities, so he is faced with serious and difficult decisions. That's why humans get those things called ulcers.

Sometimes the only solution is not only to own the property under these difficult conditions, but to go out and obtain a deer lease on another property. I will talk about leases in another letter, but believe me, a human will suffer from schizophrenia when he owns a nice property with a good deer population and then has to lease another property where the deer are never as plentiful or of good quality.

Landless humans always look covetously at those of their species who do own deer property. They just don't realize the difficulties.

I'll write again soon, and explain to you what other methods humans may use to find good places to hunt and still avoid problems with public lands.

Love,

Buck

To Lease or Not to Lease

Deer Dad:

Well, Dad, I have been explaining the problems of hunters finding a good place to hunt. We know public hunting presents problems for hunters. I also told you about some of the difficulties in owning his own land. How about a hunter purchasing a hunting lease?

Just like everything else in this world, leasing has both advantages and disadvantages. Let's look at some of both. I really can't explain the whole story to you—it would take a book, if not a series of books, to cover all the details. I will try to cover the highlights.

The main advantage of purchasing a lease is that it gives the hunter the right to hunt game (the species to be determined and included as part of the lease) without interference by other hunters. That's the most important part, pure and simple. Essential to the quality of the lease, and included in the cost, are the details associated with the deal the hunter makes with the landowner. Every disadvantage to any lease (besides the exorbitant price) relates to the details of the negotiation and the hunting rights either included or excluded in the contract.

If he is a serious hunter, he should pay careful consideration to the details of the lease, attempting to cover all the potential possibilities both known and unknown in order to provide the best contract. If the landowner is serious, he should negotiate a contract that clearly outlines all the possibilities that may develop in the relationship with his hunters so that there will be no surprises later on and so that he can receive a fair price for the lease.

Unfortunately, this is not often done. Most landowners pride themselves on their ability to judge cattle and people. Based on the concept that their word is their bond, they often believe a deal sealed with a handshake is enough. It is not! The best leases are carefully written to include all details before the deal is final. That way, a mutually agreeable relationship between both parties can last for years. Other-wise, discontent and arguments usually ensue.

What are some of the elements that should be covered in the lease, clearly spelled out and mutually agreeable? A lease is a negotiated document and there needs to be give and take in the negotiation. I will list some of the questions that need to be answered. I will be neither presumptuous nor crazy to try to answer the questions for either the hunter or the landowner. Remember, I'm in the middle and the actual object of these negotiations. I have my own bias about the whole thing.

How big is the property included in this lease?

Does the lease include the whole property or just part?

How is the property fenced?

Will the lease be shared with others?

How many hunters (guns) can be brought on the lease?

Will the lease span the entire hunting season? The entire year?

What species of game can be shot on the property?

Is any part of the property "off limits"?

What facilities on the property can be used (ie. water, buildings, etc.)?

Is the lease renewable year after year?

Can the property be used for any other activities during the year (ie. picnics with family, scouting)?

What are the "house rules"?

Hunting leases are contracts, just like any other contract. Both parties need to understand that leases are serious documents and their particulars must be followed. Similarly, cancellation of the leases must be possible for both parties. Cancellation clauses should be included in the lease and the reasons why cancellation may be demanded included as well.

The stronger the lease, the better the relationship between the hunter and landowner. If the lease is done correctly, many wonderful relationships will be established that will last for years.

That's enough about leases for today. I will write again soon to discuss other options of finding a place to hunt.

Love,

Buck

I Had a Friend

Deer Dad:

This is another letter in my series on where to hunt. Assuming a hunter does not want to hunt on public land (a safety decision), and does not want to figure out how to own his own hunting land (a genetic or matrimonial decision), and does not want to buy a lease (a financial decision), what has he got left? Actually, not much, except his incessant ingenuity.

As a last resort, but not as a good long term method, he could ask permission to hunt on someone else's land or lease. I will admit that this once worked very well, before landowners realized what their game was worth. Times are different now. Most landowners understand that wildlife is a good cash crop. They will protect it. I would strongly advise a hunter to avoid walking up to some stranger whose property is known for its superior game and asking permission to hunt. It probably won't work and will just raise some question about his sanity.

Just about the only other alternative is to ask permission to hunt from a friend who has such a property. The would-be hunter had better be ready for a variety of reactions from his friend when he tries this option.

First of all, he could lose his friend. Dad, I already warned you how covetous most landowners are of their game. I suppose the landowner wouldn't treat his friend as an illegal hunter (more about this in another letter,) but he may not consider him far from it. It could end a beautiful relationship.

On the other hand, the hunter may just be lucky and get an invitation out of his request. If he does, he should take warning. He has been given a gift of unsurpassed generosity and he had better treat it as such. While on the property, he better demonstrate his best manners. He better do everything in his power to get along and be as solicitous as possible to his host. He should be considerate of his every whim and cater to him. Pamper him. He should try to throw some business his way, or in some way return the favor.

Most importantly, the guest must make sure he clearly understands his host's rules for the hunt and what kind of game he will be
allowed to hunt. My best advice to the lucky hunter is: DON'T
MESS UP. That is, of course, if he wants to hunt on the friend's
property again.

I knew of one landowner who had a prize buffalo on the ranch.
A family pet, this buffalo was a gift to the rancher from an old and
dear friend. Sure enough, one season a guest hunter got so excited
when he saw the buffalo that he shot it, thinking it was some
strange kind of deer (I will write to you about Buck Fever).

There wasn't much the landowner could do except make the
hunter field dress the buffalo. That must have been a sight to see.
Invitations to hunt, obtained in any fashion, should be treated with
the highest regard. The guest must not be a boor and ask to bring a
friend. He should not come unprepared, without a rifle or some
other essential piece of equipment. He should try to be a gracious
guest. Then he might get invited back.

Actually, Dad, the care and feeding of a host/landowner is so
important that I will devote an entire letter to that subject.
Meanwhile, take care of yourself, and be careful.

Love,

Buck

Care and Feeding of the Landowner

Deer Dad:

I hope you are well. Deer have to understand and use every technique available in order to survive. One of these techniques is psychology. This is especially true when dealing with the landowner.

No matter who you are, hunter or huntee, you have to always be cognizant of the landowner. The landowner is clearly the most important cog in the wheel of hunting fortune. Everybody better be nice to the landowner. God knows, I am. I go out of my way to be loyal to him. Of course, there are landowners and there are landowners. Some are really honorable; others can be difficult. Some will listen to reason, and others know it all and you can't tell them a thing.

Dad, I know that you know how to treat the landowner, but I thought I would review some of the things I have learned.

First of all from the deer's side of the ranch I always try to please the landowner. He wants to know that he has a superior herd on his property. After all, he spent a considerable amount of money, time, and heartache developing a trophy herd. I want him to know he was successful. He built a game proof fence around the whole property. He achieved a proper buck to doe ratio and then had the patience to wait several years while culling the herd to let the young bucks develop into mature trophies. He also endured the jokes and criticisms of his neighbors who thought he was crazy. He showed them; now they're jealous and several years behind him in game management. I will write more about game management techniques in future letters.

In order to keep the landowner friendly and on my side, I take great pains to curry favor with him. Actually, it doesn't take very much effort. I do go out of my way to let him catch glimpses of me from time to time. He knows I'm here. He knows where I live, generally. He knows I am a trophy, but that I'm also smart and not about to let him or someone else stumble onto me or catch me without a great fight. In fact, I know he cares about me. He spends time scouting around in my pasture. He has that longing look in his eyes. I know he wants me. For that, I am thankful. After all, everybody wants to be wanted. But, my landowner knows how to wait. Patience is not a universal human quality, but my landowner has patience.

As far as humans are concerned, the care and feeding of landowners is a much more complicated matter. It really makes no difference whether the hunter is a guest, lease holder, or poacher; he better keep an eye on the landowner at all times. After all, the landowner is his ticket to the hunt.

Hunters need to be friendly; they need to show respect and at least pretend to heed the advice of the landowner. Actually, if the hunter is smart, he better do more than pretend to heed the advice. He must pay very close attention to the advice and follow it to the letter. After all, who knows the local territory better than the man who spends most of his time on the property?

What the landowner really wants and, in fact, what he deserves, is for the hunter to use the property as agreed upon either in the lease or in the invitation and not do anything to spoil the rest of the land or its inhabitants. In every case I have seen, the landowner truly loves the land he owns and wants to protect it and prolong its productivity. He does not care for individuals who invade his land and destroy it. Destructive activity is understandably infuriating to the person who has put so much of himself and his resources into the land. Abuse of it will cause serious unhappiness to the landowner.

The landowner's unhappiness may take many forms. The guest may not be invited back. The lessee may lose his lease. If the hunter is really troublesome or does something illegal who knows what may be his fate. I have heard of strange retaliations to some illegal acting or ungrateful humans.

The hunter had better not risk making the landowner unhappy. All he has to do is treat the landowner's property as he would his own. He should protect it and not harm it.

The net result of a proper attitude is a continued good relationship with the single most important individual in the hunting chain—the landowner. The stronger the chain, the stronger the future hunting.

Enough about how to care for the landowner. I think I'll end now and let you get some rest. I hope your eyes are not too tired from reading all these letters. I do find a certain relaxation in spending time writing to you.

Love,

Buck

Bucks and Does and Does and Does

Deer Dad:

I hope you are well. In my last letter I reminded you how we have to practice the science of Psychology. We also have to study the science of Game Management.

Deer understood the principles of game management long before humans. We have managed to keep most of the principles secret. I know they can do us harm if the humans learn all our secrets. There are some secrets I wish they would learn, especially the ones dealing with game management.

I have been spending a great deal of time thinking about these letters I have been writing to you. There have been several of them and some contain valuable information for humans as well as for deer. In fact, I have been trying to decide whether I should find a way to pass this information on to humans so they can improve their hunting skills and game management techniques. Both deer and hunters would benefit from thoughtful planning in both areas. I feel this would actually help deer in the long run. I might even receive some credit for my contribution from among our relatives.

You can help if you could find a way to leave these letters where humans can find them. Then we can watch for improvements in their techniques. If such an experiment is successful, I will be very happy and will consider expanding the educational concept into a book or something.

I digress. The subject of this letter is supposed to be game management. There have been many myths perpetrated on humans by their fellows. For example: "The check is in the mail," or "Taxes are going to go down next year." The biggest myth and the one that has had the most impact on deer management is, "Don't shoot the does."

This myth has been passed on from father to son for generations. At first glance, the inexperienced might see some merit to the concept that no doe should ever be shot. Does are, after all, the fawn-making machines. Without them there would be no new deer.

That's true, but when you consider deer management in the broad sense, such a practice will eventually give you many more does than bucks.

The other commonly voiced reason for keeping all the does is that a buck can service many does during a rut and therefore the owner is doing the bucks a disservice if he doesn't have many does around for them. Well, this is true, and I for one do appreciate the rut as one of the greatest benefits of being a deer. Good management calls for a program designed to produce the best quality population which must include an appropriate number of quality bucks. I will have to learn to share.

What is the proper buck to doe ratio? If I told the average hunter it was close to one to one, he would cringe and call me stupid. Believe me or not, it would be better one to one than what I often see of 10 or 20 to one. One to one is a good number to aim for.

Of course, it's far more complicated than that. The proper buck to doe ratio must fit in with all the other management tools that must be set in place to produce quality deer.

There are a large number of factors that are all interrelated and must be considered simultaneously when planning a whitetail management program. An appropriate buck to doe ratio with quality animals in the herd is the ultimate goal. The path to get to that goal is often long and usually requires a considerable financial investment. Since more and more landowners are realizing the potential value in a superior herd, they are increasingly willing to make that investment and develop long range plans to produce a superior return on their money.

I, a mere deer, would not presume to lecture on the way to plan for such an outcome. What I will do, Dad, is report to you some of my own feelings on the techniques I have seen used to develop a trophy caliber game program, the kind of program any self-respecting landowner would be proud to have.

Let me state, here and now, that planning and developing such a program will not conflict with the other interests of ranchers and landowners. Cattle, agriculture, oil production, and other activities can all coexist. So, deer can get along well with many other land uses, and priorities should not conflict at any time.

Love,

Buck

"Don't Fence Me In"

Deer Dad:

Here is another letter about game management. I know you have heard cowboys sitting around the campfire singing that old Texas song, "*Don't Fence Me In.*" I think it must have been written by a deer.

I have to talk about fences if I am going to talk about game management. There are fences, and there are fences. Most fences humans see in whitetail country are the three or four strand barbed wire fences that line the highways. They are designed for cattle and work well. They do not fence in deer. We can easily go over them or under them—so can most game. It is more difficult planning effective game management using low fences.

If a landowner really wants to develop a quality herd, then he has to fence his property with an eight foot high, game proof fence. This will serve two main purposes: keep his high quality (eventually) game in and keep low quality and unwanted animals out. The basic assumption is that he is fencing enough property to make it worthwhile. The size of the fenced property depends upon how many deer he wants to keep and how many deer per acre his property can support. More about that later. Obviously, one hundred acres in far west Texas is not the same as one hundred acres in downtown Houston.

There are certain disadvantages to a landowner in building a game-proof fence around property. One is that it is rather expensive, at least initially, before he has the quality deer he desires. Unfortunately he has to have the fence before he can have the quality deer. While it does represent a large investment, a high fence will pay off in the long run.

The second major disadvantage of a high fence is that any animals currently harvested behind such a fence will not qualify for inclusion in the Boone and Crockett record book. The Boone and Crockett Society has kept records for many years listing the largest and best quality animals of many species along with the names of the hunters who shot them. Best quality is determined by a sophisticated (read that complicated) scoring system that includes several measurements of the animal's antlers. Along with the measurements, there are rules that must be followed including a proscription against shooting an animal within an enclosure. This rule, designed to eliminate the practice of "growing" deer in pens just for the record books, makes some sense when fencing in only a few acres. If the rancher is considering fencing in several thousand acres, then these fences should not interfere with the free movement of the game.

Since most deer remain homebodies, rarely traveling more than a mile or two from home, most deer would probably never even see a fence built around a few thousand acres. Nevertheless, the Boone and Crockett rule is still present and must be considered. It is not likely the average or superior hunter would mind the slight inconvenience of being unable to register in the record books. Moreover, since only a very few bucks would qualify for such a record anyway, the advantages of fencing outweigh the disadvantages. Hopefully, some day the Boone and Crockett humans will relent a bit on this rather stringent rule and develop a fair fence regulation. If enough hunters lobby the Society, they may be successful.

Then, the bottom line advice to the landowner on fences is to build one if he can afford it. He should consider building one even if he cannot afford it. He should remember an alternative to building one is to own a piece of property sufficiently large to negate the need for a fence because he has enough control by size alone. As an alternative, he should get together with his neighbors, who all appreciate the advantages of game management, so that together they have enough property to avoid the need of such a high fence. Also, he should try to be in the middle of this group. The landowners on the edges will still have the problem of needing a fence. If this sounds just like a big "pyramid club," I guess it is, but it's the only way to do it correctly. Since most landowners are almost always on the edge of something, it is usually best to bite the bullet and build a fence. Biting the bullet isn't so bad when you consider the alternative use of bullets, which is what we deer face all the time.

I hope this letter gets into the right hands after you read it. Don't eat this one. Let it lie around where some human may find it, perhaps in a bookstore in some shopping mall.

Love,

Buck

Acre by Acre

Deer Dad:

I've talked about fences. I also have to talk about what is being fenced. It is extremely important to realize that we deer (as in almost every species I know) like to eat. If we don't eat, we starve. If we starve, we cheat the humans out of what they want most—us. Therefore, it's in everyone's best interest not to let this happen.

Humans are very aware that it takes a certain amount of land and the food contained therein to support a specific number of cattle. Put too many cattle on the land and they will not do well. Put too few and valuable property is wasted. Humans can cheat a little by providing extra food for their cattle and get a few extra cattle on the same piece of land. Actually, they could do this for us, also, but not as easily. We eat different foods.

The same rules that apply to cattle apply to us. The number of deer an acre of land can support depends upon a variety of factors related to the types of food available as well as the type of cover, water, minerals, etc. It is really beyond the scope of this letter to detail the exact formulas for the best number of deer per acre with all the variations and possibilities available in this country. Valuable information can be obtained in every geographical area from local and state experts who deal in wildlife management, so there is really no excuse for a landowner to remain ignorant about this important information.

The first step is to determine the number of deer a particular range can support. The goal then is to restrict the deer population to that number and to remember to aim for a buck to doe ratio of one to one or thereabouts.

If the landowner is successful, what has he accomplished? He has provided the best possible nutrition for the deer on his property. This will minimize death by nature, which is not at all pleasant. Dying by starvation is not the best way to depart this earth. If I may wax philosophical for a minute, it seems to a lowly animal like me that a sudden end by a hunter's bullet is far preferable to starvation.

If we are given the best possible nutrition, then my friends and neighbors and I will grow to our maximal potential both in body weight (for the meat hunters) and in antler development (for the trophy hunters). We will develop into a truly superior balanced herd rather than a group of scrawny, overpopulated does with an assortment of spikes (more about them later) instead of quality bucks.

We certainly have come a long way in just a few letters. We understand our goals. We know about fences and deer population configurations, and we are now ready to individualize these concepts to our own particular needs. My God, I sound like the landowner. I think I am making a great mistake giving away all these secrets. Then again, all this is well known and easily available to even the casual human reader. As I mentioned in a previous letter, if the humans learn it from me at least it will have the ring of authority and they will believe it. Now that I've gone this far, I guess I will continue in future letters with the next steps.

Love,

Buck

1, 2, 3, 4...

Deer Dad:

In previous letters I have outlined some of the steps a landowner needs to consider when planning for a trophy herd of deer. I have discussed high fences, buck to doe ratios, and estimation of the number of deer a piece of property can support. The next step is of utmost importance but often overlooked.

Once the landowner accurately determines the number of deer he wants, he must then determine the number of deer he has. Obvious, right? Not to all humans. Actually, a game survey should be conducted annually.

Of course, there are many ways to do this and not all are equal in quality. Surveys can be conducted by walking around counting, by driving around counting, or by flying around counting. In all cases, it requires counting.

A landowner could count one of his 5,000 acres and multiply the number of deer he sees by 5,000. He could count 2,500 of his 5,000 acres and multiply by 2. Or, he could count all 5,000 acres and realize that he is still missing many animals and his results are just estimates. Annual counting of the entire property will give the best results over a period of time and doing it by air, where local terrain permits, is probably the most accurate way to accomplish this chore.

Actually, its not a chore at all. If the landowner takes movies or videos while counting from the air, the result will be a wonderful pictorial review of the topography and wildlife of his property that he will spend countless hours watching with great pleasure.

He should be warned, however, that the trophy animals he sees in the aerial survey will completely disappear come next hunting season even though this superb scouting method clearly demonstrates the deer activity. This is particularly vexing to him when he remembers that, in general, deer will remain in the same general vicinity throughout their lives.

Now of course the rut, a fire, or some other natural or manmade disaster (ie. a highway or oil well), may result in deer movement, but it really takes quite a change to move the deer.

Anyway, once the survey is complete, even though it is only an estimate, if it was done carefully it will be fairly accurate. If the ideal number of bucks and does is known, and the actual number is also known, then it's a simple calculation to determine the number and sex of those deer that need to be harvested.

In a future letter, Dad, I will describe which are the best deer to harvest under these circumstances. Since I have undertaken to reveal the innermost secrets of game management, at great personal risk, it becomes very important to me to be sure that the landowner takes every precaution to ensure a good end result with a superior herd of trophy deer. This will better our species and will make the revelations worthwhile. Since I believe I could qualify as a trophy myself, I would like to see the best possible selection process to enhance future generations.

Love,

Buck

Who Goes?

Deer Dad:

Well, Dad, my series of letters on game management is just about over. There is only one more subject to consider. The landowner has decided to build a fence. He has come to grips with the age old tradition about not killing does. He has decided to aim for an appropriate buck to doe ratio and has determined how many deer the range can support.

Not only that, he has taken a good deer census and knows reasonably accurately how many animals he has on the property.

All he has to decide now is how many and who go. Calculating the number of animals he needs to shoot is easy. Determining which ones is not so easy. There are a few rules of thumb he can follow.

First of all which deer does he want to keep? He wants to keep all bucks that are of good quality for their age class. It's difficult to tell the age of a deer even when he is field dressed and in position to be examined closely. We will talk about determining age in a later letter, primarily aimed at dentists. Nevertheless, the landowner wants to keep the best bucks of each age class around and particularly most of the middle age classes.

It's even harder to tell the age of a female deer than a male deer, but the main thing is he wants to keep the most productive does around, which are usually the ones in the middle age classes. Remember, this is not a time for chivalry. The doe count will dictate the number needed. The hunter must not chicken out.

Very old deer should be harvested. They will die of starvation in the winter and be less prolific in the rut, so their value to the herd is minimal.

How about spikes? Spikes are deer with a single point on each side. There are many stories about spikes. One, they are just very young deer and will grow fine antlers next year. Two, they are good potential bucks who just didn't get enough to eat during the antler growing season. Three, they are genetically inferior animals of any age who will remain spikes forever.

39

All three stories could or could not be true, depending on the individual situation. In general, spikes should be culled from the herd. In fact, if the house rules call for hunters to shoot only a single buck each, then an additional buck should be awarded for any hunter who shoots a spike.

BUT BEWARE!! The hunter should not confuse a young branch antlered buck with a spike. It is essential to study the antler characteristics carefully before deciding a spike is truly a spike. A small branch antlered buck will grow into a nice mature buck in future years and should not, I repeat should not, be taken. He should be left alone to grow up.

If an animal is obviously diseased, he or she should be culled from the herd. Any animal with a deformity that indicates he will not survive a hard winter should be sacrificed. By the way, a broken antler does not count as a deformity. A deer may have broken an antler during a fight or some other accident, but remember, antlers will be shed and a fine new set will grow next year. By the same token, a deer with a broken rack would not make a good mount and unless very old, should be left alone.

Following these practices and reducing the herd to the correct number based on all of these considerations is the first step to producing a superior herd. Good game management practices will let nothing stand in the way of success, especially ancient customs, family traditions, or hunters with "buck fever," a disease we will study in future letters.

These practices I explained are what I would do if I were a landowner interested in improving my deer. Of course, I'm not a landowner but rather a deer, so I must maintain the posture of publicly advocating just the opposite. Nevertheless, this system works.

Take care of yourself. I will write again soon.

Love,

Buck

What About Next Year

Deer Dad:

I wonder if any landowners took my advice and followed the instructions in the last several letters. If they have, they have taken the initial steps toward the development of a first class deer population. There should be just about the right number of animals on the property and just about the right sex distribution.

Of course, it may have been impossible to achieve complete success in one season. In fact, if the buck to doe ratio was so high that there were many, many more does than bucks, getting to a one to one ratio may take several seasons of planning the deer harvest very carefully. Achieving the correct total number for the land is most important to produce good growth and minimize starvation. It can be done fairly rapidly, but it doesn't make sense to harvest huge numbers of does just because there are only one or two bucks on the ranch. Remember that there is an approximate fifty-fifty chance that a pregnant doe will give birth to a male or female. Twins are common. The landowner must understand that he may have to have one or more seasons of harvesting only does to eventually achieve a good ratio.

Once the correct number and sex distribution is achieved, then additional steps need to be taken annually to make certain the numbers are maintained and the quality of the herd improved.

An annual count is desirable, but two years of management can be done on one year's count. It's expensive, but it's worth it. The landowner can then be sure that he has an appropriate number of animals and he will know how many to harvest next season.

An accurate census will also give some information about the condition of the deer and the quality of the bucks, their size, antler configuration, and the sex ratio—all essential information to compare year after year.

The fawn drop will not be one hundred percent successful. Some newborn deer will not survive. Survival rates fluctuate from year to year and even from area to area in the same year. Those that do survive will have to be nourished and will need adequate food supplies in order that their growth can be maximized.

Once the calculations are made as to the best numbers to harvest next season, then common sense and willpower are required to make sure only those numbers are, in fact, taken. I can assure all landowners that as soon as the appropriate number of deer are harvested, more quality bucks will appear and it will take great moral fortitude to refrain from getting "just one more deer." In fact, I will let you in on a secret. The deer already know the numbers and we trophies wait to appear until after the threat to our own longevity is gone.

I think I have spent enough time on the fundamentals of game management. I know this is not a complete report on all the intricacies. It would take many books to adequately cover the subject. Not only that, new information is constantly being discovered. A truly interested and committed landowner will get more information and expert advice. I do hope this is enough to motivate some of them into action.

Love,

Buck

It's that Time Again

Deer Dad:

Here we go again. The new hunting season is rapidly approaching. How can I tell? Well, there are many ways to tell. First of all, I could look at a calendar. The season is usually the same time every fall. I could also tell by how I feel. My antlers are growing nicely and the velvet is just about gone. Also, there is definitely a chill in the evening air that tells me the weather is getting colder.

These are not the best ways to tell when hunting season approaches. The best way to tell is to watch the activities humans are performing to get ready for the new season. There is scurrying about setting up feeders, checking and erecting new blinds, fixing up the hunting cabins, and many other things.

It's interesting, Dad. The one thing they are not doing is any scouting to see where we are and what we are doing. They already have taken a survey, but nobody has spent extra time walking around and looking or just sitting and looking. Oh well, I suppose they may learn someday.

Now that the humans are right in the middle of all these preparations, I thought I would write you a few letters and describe what they are doing. I think I also may include how to prepare correctly so that if any human ever reads these letters he will know that there is a right way.

In this letter, I thought I'd talk about feeders. Feeders are very clever contraptions. They consist of a few mechanical parts designed to work together to allow periodic dispersal of some type of food (usually corn) to supplement our diet.

Don't get me wrong, Dad. Landowners and hunters are interested in our general status of nutrition (ha, ha), but they are much more interested in our general status of location. They believe that if they put out feeders in strategic locations on their property we will be attracted to these locations during the hunting season so that we can be shot more easily.

In fact, they are correct. We do have this damnable trait of becoming used to certain activities. I think humans call them habits. Unfortunately, we can be trained in this regard, and, if the feeders are well placed and set up long before the season begins or better still left up all year long, then we will develop the habit of visiting them frequently. We will especially do this if our regular food is in short supply.

Of course, it is in our own best interests to remember to do this feeding at night, when we are reasonably safe from hunters (if not from poachers). Unfortunately, we often forget this simple principle and it means our end.

Anyway, Dad, a feeder has to have only a few parts. It needs some type of reservoir to hold enough food so that the landowner doesn't have to fill it often. It has to have a mechanism to disperse the food periodically, usually a few times a day, in appropriate quantities. There has to be some type of timing mechanism, usually run by batteries, to start the dispersal system. Also, it should be raised above the ground so that the food is dispersed over a wide area below and to the sides of the feeder.

Actually, it's a simple idea but, as humans are wont to do, feeders have been manufactured in all shapes, sizes, and at all different costs. All this to get the corn on the ground.

From the landowner's point of view, feeders are all right but far from perfect. Remember that corn is not only considered a delicacy by us but by many other animals as well. All sorts of animals and birds will come around to check out the feeder for dessert so that much of its effect may be lost. Now remember, Dad, these machines are just machines. They have been built by humans in something called a factory out of man-made materials. They break, get old, rust, and often fall down. Some landowners find them more trouble than they're worth.

Also, thank God, there are a significant and growing number of hunters who believe that use of a feeder renders the sport of deer hunting unfair. They believe that deer hunting is a contest between themselves and a very capable adversary, and they do not want to take unfair advantage of us. That's really nice, since the stakes for each side in the contest are drastically different.

If the hunter fails, he goes home, makes up a few lies about why he didn't get a deer, and has a chance to come back again another day. If the deer fails, it's gloves, dinner, and a trip to the taxidermist.

Here I go getting depressed. I'm going to end now and write you again soon about more hunting preparations.

Love,

Buck

Preparation Saves Face

Deer Dad:

Humans are odd creatures. They rarely say what they mean. Let me give you an example. These two humans were complaining about a soft drink machine that frequently took their money but did not give them a drink. One of them told the other that he wasn't angry about the money, it was the principle involved. I have learned that whenever a human says, "It isn't the money, it's the principle," it's really the money.

Human hunters say just about the same thing. When one of them shoots a mediocre to poor quality buck, they always say the same thing. "I hunt for food, not trophies." Now really. Do they expect us to believe that they would turn down a Boone and Crockett quality buck because he had a small body?

It has something to do with "face" and the human's need to save it. Humans feel the only thing worse than shooting a poor deer is to shoot no deer at all. I will admit that there are some humans who do hunt appropriately, waiting for the kind of deer they really want to shoot. I will also admit that there are some hunters who really do hunt for meat and won't shoot a buck at all, but in most instances human hunting tactics are totally irrational and purely emotional. They must have some hormonal problems that are difficult to overcome.

If humans would spend some time preparing and learning appropriate hunting methods, they would be better off. That takes time and interest. Humans are always short on both, and that works in our favor. Like most other things, hunting is 90 percent preparation and 10 percent actually hunting.

When does preparation start for the hunting season? Of course, it starts right after the end of the previous season. A hunter interested in excellence (as well as luck, which is probably more important than excellence) will begin for next year right now. First of all, as soon as he is finished using his rifle, he needs to give it proper care for its sleep during those long non-hunting months. It needs to be thoroughly cleaned, oiled, and polished. The true hunter will go one step further. He won't put the rifle away at all. Oh, he will clean it after each use, but he will use it all year long. I don't mean hunting deer out of season, but I do mean he will shoot at targets throughout the year to maintain or perfect his abilities.

There is a very old but true story about the human who got into a taxicab in New York City and asked the driver if he knew how to get to Carnegie Hall. The driver responded, "Practice, man, practice." The same is true for a deer hunter. Time spent on the range practicing is time well spent to ensure a good season next year.

Another important part of preparation for the next hunting season is physical preparation. Most hunters, in fact most humans, don't bother with this at all even though it is so important. Hunting is a vigorous outdoor sport. To do it correctly requires significant exertion. Basically, hunters have to be in good physical shape to withstand the rigors of even a partial, much less a full, hunting season. Appropriate diet and exercise during the off-season is essential. If we were in as bad physical shape as most humans are, we would have been destroyed as a species long ago.

Of course, rifle care, practice shooting and physical conditioning are only a few of the ways hunters need to prepare for the hunting season. I will describe more of them in future letters.

Take care of yourself. Remember hunter preparations mean fall will soon be here with winter to follow. Try to eat a good diet so you can survive next winter.

Love,

Buck

Hunting is Expensive

Deer Dad:

Humans use this stuff called money. I have watched them many times. They take little pieces of paper with funny printing on them and give them to each other. Apparently, in exchange for the paper, they get things they want. Sometimes, but not often, they use little pieces of metal.

When a human hunter wants to get hunting equipment, he uses this money, but he always seems to use much more of it than humans use for other things. In fact, I heard some hunters talking once and they said that humans spend more money on hunting than they do on any other participatory sport. There seems to be some need that hunters have to own more expensive and elaborate hunting equipment than their friends. A rivalry seems to develop between hunters to outdo each other. I suppose they think if they purchase more expensive equipment they will be better hunters or have more hunting success. In fact, that is usually not true. It is not the quality of the equipment that spells success but the quality of the hunter.

Now, Dad, I know you realize that there does have to be a certain basic quality of equipment involved with successful hunting, but cost alone is not the only way to select the proper equipment. I have seen some hunting rifles that are loaded with fancy carving and engraving on the weapon, but they don't shoot straight. I have seen telescopic sights that have many fancy features on them such as zoom lenses and distance markers, that are so complicated to use the average hunter misses the shot just trying to deal with focusing and using the sight.

I have heard hunters sitting around their hunting dens comparing the number and cost of their rifles with each other in a contest to determine who has spent the most on his hobby. You know, Dad, it is true that different hunting locations and purposes will call for different types of weapons, but it does not follow that rifles should be considered "disposable," to be used once and then put away forever. In fact, hunters could probably cover most hunting situations with only a very few types of rifles. There is a great deal to be said for using a single weapon as much as possible and becoming totally familiar with that rifle and its peculiarities.

How is a hunter, especially a neophyte, supposed to choose from the huge amount of equipment available the proper equipment at reasonable costs? The best way to do it is with education. As a matter of fact, education will generally maximize a human's hunting success. It's well worth the time it takes.

Seeking expert advice will generally pay off in the long run. Of course, the secret is in accurately identifying an expert. Experts are usually not friends. They usually are available, although they often charge for their advice. I will write a separate letter about experts and advice. The important thing to remember here is that there is no need to run out and purchase the first available piece of equipment but to take adequate time, learn what is needed, and shop around before buying.

No matter what the hunter may think, the sport is expensive. He should remember it will always be cheaper to buy beef in the supermarket than to go out and try to stock the larder in the field.

Dad, don't worry about money. We don't really need much of it since there is no place to spend it where we live.

Love,

Buck

Weapons to Fear

Deer Dad:

I hope this letter finds you well. I found a human book the other day, one which I have never seen before. It's called a dictionary. The author is some fellow named Webster. I couldn't really understand the plot, but believe me it had some cast of characters. Actually, I studied it quite carefully. It is not a novel at all, but rather a list of all the words humans use and what they mean. I found the word "hunt" in the book. Knowing what the word really means sheds a light on many of our problems. The word "hunt" has two meanings. The first is "to kill or catch game for food or sport." The second is "to try to find; search, seek." Now, isn't that interesting! Hunters actually have a choice when they go hunting. The choice they make will determine which type of weapon they use during the hunt, and believe me, Dad, there are good weapons and bad weapons from our point of view.

Not to make this letter too long since I know you get weary from reading long letters, I thought I would tell you in this letter about the weapons we need to fear and in the next letter the weapons we can love.

First of all, we have the rifle. A diabolical instrument, it can shoot a small, pointed piece of metal with great speed a very long distance with tremendous power so that if an object is hit it can easily be destroyed, even if the object is a living thing.

The point is that there are a large variety of rifles, all having different sizes, power, and something called "ballistic characteristics." Humans have to make decisions about which type to buy (or borrow) in order to hunt. Humans often have a problem choosing. That is not only true for rifles. They have difficulties choosing many other things. One of the most difficult things they have to choose is a wife. They often make mistakes in these kind of decisions. To err when choosing a rifle is not so bad, he can just choose another one. To err in choosing a wife creates all sorts of problems. That's another story.

Rifles are made by several different companies. The first thing a hunter has to do is choose a particular brand. It turns out that several of the companies make very fine rifles and as long as the hunter chooses a "name brand," he shouldn't get into trouble. It's when he starts to look for bargains with "off-name" brands or no-name brands that he runs the risk of getting stuck. There is a human expression called "caveat emptor." It means if the deal sounds too good, it is, and it's better left alone.

The caliber or size of the rifle is important. Shortly after humans found out how to make rifles and bullets to shoot out of them, they discovered that if they made several sizes, and told hunters that each size was special and necessary, then they could sell many more rifles. Actually, Dad, there are differences in the different sizes. The real question is are there really significant differences in the often minute differences in sizes?

If the hunter is after small game, like squirrels, then using a large caliber rifle like a "30-06" is clearly inappropriate. It will totally destroy the animal rather than preserve it for use. On the other hand, if he uses a "22" caliber rifle to shoot larger animals like us that is also inappropriate since the bullet is too small and will not kill us cleanly, much less kill us at all. Oh, don't get me wrong! A small caliber rifle can do damage to large animals and might even kill them, but it is much more likely to only wound large animals and cause suffering without producing hunting success.

Besides the caliber of the rifle there are other considerations. Some rifles change bullets by a "bolt action" device that gets rid of the used cartridge casing. Others use a lever device to do the same thing. The bolt type is probably better for deer hunting and ease in taking that second or third shot. There are also "semi-automatic" types that allow the hunter to shoot continuously each time he pulls the trigger with the bullets advancing automatically. There are even some rifles that shoot several bullets by just pulling the trigger once, but they are generally illegal in most places. These are very dangerous but not so much for us as for other humans. Humans favor using these types on one another rather than on animals.

All rifles use bullets which actually do the killing. Some hunters buy these bullets in the same kind of store where they purchased their rifle. Some hunters, on the other hand, become very fanatical about the bullets themselves and insit theat they can produce better bullets with more consistent quality than the manufacturers who have large machines and extensive quality control measures. These humans purchase expensive equipment and materials and then spend hours and hours loading their own ammunition. They claim it's a great hobby and significantly improves their shooting accuracy. Who am I to dispute them?

Once the decision is reached about the type of rifle and bullets the hunter will use, he has another decision to make. You see, Dad, shooting the rifle is one thing. Hitting what he is shooting at is entirely another matter. There are little gadgets on the top of the rifle called sights and the hunter must line these up with the target when aiming the weapon. Many hunters, choosing to take advantage of us, use modern human technology by augmenting their aiming capability. They attach a telescopic device to the rifle to magnify the target and aid in aiming. Telescopic sights, usually called "scopes," come in different types and sizes. The hunter will have to choose how much he wants to magnify the target. Of course, the more magnification, the bigger the scope, the narrower the field of view, and the more expensive the purchase. As you might expect, there are some hunters who can't make up their minds what size scope they want. For these individuals, there is a device called a "variable scope." These scopes have the ability to vary the magnification so that the hunter can look close or far away. The usual scenario is that while the hunter is manipulating the scope and fiddling with the levers, gears, and what have you, we have a good chance to get away. As you know, hunters are strange folk who try to make things as hard as they can for themselves. If they would just keep it simple, they would do much better.

There are also other variations in weapons. In some places hunters use shotguns instead of rifles, but they use "slugs" or large pieces of metal instead of pellets. These shotguns are especially good for short range. Speaking of short range, there are some hunters that actually use bows and arrows like the old-time Indians used. Dad, this is a very difficult way to hunt, and the hunter who uses this method must really be skilled, not only in use of the bow, but also in his ability to track, stalk, and still hunt. You see, the distance an arrow will be effective is very short, and the hunter really has to get close to his target. Naturally, that gives us an advantage since any noise, scent or visual identification of the hunter will allow us to be long gone.

This is a long letter, and really gives only a superficial description of some weapons. Humans have written entire books about this subject, and I really don't want to repeat all of that. This is just to give you a brief idea of the problem. If you want to know more about it, I will get you some literature provided by all the "experts."

Take care of yourself. I will write again soon about other types of weapons hunters can use that we deer really like.

Love,

Buck

Weapons to Love

Deer Dad:

I hope you are well. I am worried that I caused you to strain your eyes reading my last letter. I know it was a long one, but the subject was important. I want to write to you today about some other types of weapons, very different from the last ones because they simply record events without any destructive potential. Some hunters use these non-destructive weapons exclusively and others, part time. Either way, these weapons don't hurt anybody.

One of these "happy weapons" is a gadget called a camera. It is a funny little box that has a big nose on it with a glass middle. The hunter looks through it and pushes a little button. That's all! Nothing comes out the end, and nothing hurts us. I glimpsed some of the "pictures" this camera takes and it's like what you see, frozen onto a piece of paper. It's amazing how close the hunter can get with the camera and how big he can make the pictures.

There is another type of camera that actually takes pictures and makes them move. I'm not really sure how it works, but the end result is that the hunter can make a visual record of the place where he points the camera. He can see us running or whatever.

Thirdly, there is a device called binoculars. These don't make a picture, but they do make things very far away seem very close. The hunter can use these to see great distances. Some hunters use them alone, others use them with rifles. They are quite indispensable in the hunting process. There are different types of binoculars. Some focus very far and some not so far. The problem with them is that the farther away they focus, the narrower view they get and many things that are just outside the field of vision may be missed.

Now, Dad, there are certain advantages to using these types of weapons. First of all, they are usually less expensive than rifles. They are much safer, safer for us but also safer for the humans. Hunters find it much harder to kill each other with a camera. Hunters can get good records of trophy deer and don't have to worry about field dressing. You know how messy that can get!

There are disadvantages for the hunter as well. There is no trophy, there is no meat, and there is a certain disdain, however misplaced, evidenced by other hunters about using cameras.

Then there is the question of game management. There is a very common argument used by hunters to explain to non-hunters why they participate in this sport. Since it's well recognized that only a certain number of deer can survive in a given area, then it follows that a hunter is actually doing the deer (plural) a favor by killing them. After all, isn't it better to have a quick end than to die of starvation?

Actually, Dad, there is some truth to this argument. If the hunter carefully manages the herd on his property and harvests just the right amount of deer each year following all the rules I have written to you about, then it does make sense. Therefore, in consideration of the herd, hunting is an important game management tool. You and I just have to remember not to let it be us.

Love,

Buck

Better Dressed is
Better than Field Dressed

Deer Dad:

I don't remember much about my childhood, but I do vaguely remember that story you told me that was passed down through the ages about why humans wear clothes. You do remember, don't you?

There were just two of them and something about an apple. Ever since then, humans have been the only species to wear clothes. Now, of course, they can't do without them, especially in the cold weather. I have seen various magazines around the hunter's lodge with photographs of the different types of clothing humans wear. Sometimes it's almost nothing, especially the female of the species. Those are really peculiar magazines. All of those kinds of magazines look like they have been read over and over.

Be that as it may, there are many different types of clothing humans wear. Believe me, Dad, there is correct clothing to wear while hunting. The wrong clothing can not only produce significant discomfort to the hunter but also ruin a perfectly good hunting trip.

Choosing the correct clothing requires a decision-making process that takes care and study. Not all humans have the ability to make the proper decisions at all times, and some have the propensity to make the wrong decisions consistently (I read that in a psychology book once.)

Here are some of the factors that hunters must consider when choosing the proper clothing. First of all, the hunter has to evaluate the weather. Will it be hot, warm, cool, cold, or all of the above? There are some humans who specialize in predicting the weather. They are called meteorologists. The good news is that they can predict the weather. The bad news is that they are often wrong. Nevertheless, it's the best method the humans have. It is essential to choose clothing that will be appropriate for the temperature. If the hunter has to make a mistake, it's better to err on the side of warm, layered clothing suitable for cold weather. He can always take some layers off. By the way, Dad, the secret for cold weather dressing (for humans) is to wear several layers, even if the layers are of lightweight material. Air trapped between the layers serves as something called insulation. It is much like our coat in this regard.

The weather can be warm or cold, but the hunter must also remember the sun. If the sun is shining brightly, then some form of protection will be required. I will talk more about this in a future letter.

We have to discuss the question of rain. If the hunter prepares for it, the rain will never come. If he does not, a hurricane is guaranteed. The secret is that the hunter must make sure that he does not water his grass or wash his car before he leaves for the hunt. Also, he must bring appropriate rain or water-repellent clothing with him. This will also ensure that the rain will not appear.

Choice of clothing should also consider skin protection. There are many, many things in deer country that could tear up unprotected skin. Practically every bush, tree, cactus, rock, and every other piece of nature is designed to injure a human. Long sleeved shirts, full legged pants, hats, and gloves are essential.

What about camouflage? I am told that stores specializing in hunting equipment (and even those that do not) are amply supplied with clothing and hunting equipment with camouflage colorations so that we (the deer) can't see them (the hunters.) I'm not sure if human scientists ever really proved that we can't see camouflage. Camouflage became very popular during the human wars so that one human could hide from another. Well, Dad, you and I certainly know whether we can see through "camo" or not, but don't worry, I have no intention of sharing this with any human that might find this letter. Anyway, it's of little consequence since we also can smell and hear them quite easily. Besides, I have to be very careful not to destroy a large segment of the human economy.

Humans had best remember that "camo" does work for them, and if they decide to hunt in a public area or even a private area, they had best consider making themselves as conspicuous as possible to each other. Clothing should be made either totally or partially of very bright orange. This color can be seen easily for fairly long distances. Since deer generally do not wear such clothing, it should serve to identify one human to another and prevent tragedy.

One other thing: even clothing that answers all of the possibilities I have mentioned in this letter can still present problems for hunters. One of the reasons humans make so much noise when they walk about hunting is that the motion of their bodies causes their clothes to make sounds, especially when two pieces rub against each other. One way to minimize this problem is to wear clothing made out of wool instead of those manmade plastic materials. The natural (read that animal-made—and therefore good) fibers are much more quiet. The wool is also more comfortable and will absorb human body moisture more easily.

That brings us to footwear. Humans don't have hooves. They have very soft, usually flat, feet and they don't even walk on their toes. They have to protect these rather delicate appendages. They wear other animal products made out of leather. Leather is animal skin tanned and constructed to cover the foot and lower leg. Shoes and boots come in various qualities with varying costs. In general, the human would be well advised to spend a little more money on his footwear and buy good quality, strong, long lasting boots that have high quality parts. The soles, upon which the human walks, should be adequate for the type of country in which the hunter will walk. The tops of the boots should reach high enough to protect the hunter against injury from the flora and fauna of the particular hunting area. If there are snakes, the boots should be quite high, coming to just below the knee. If there is moisture or water, then the boots should be waterproof. The hunter should take care to get the correct size for his foot—too tight or too loose and he will have difficulty walking. From what I have observed, sore feet are no fun.

How about socks? Socks are worn between the hunter's feet and his boots. Good socks are essential to hunter comfort and will allow him to stay out in the field (where he belongs) longer. Socks will not only protect his feet from friction of the boots, but also will add warmth and help keep his feet dry. If it's really cold, more than one pair can be worn and, believe it or not, Dad, humans have even invented socks with electric (actually battery) heating for those really cold days and nights.

After all is said and done, I must tell you the real reason humans usually buy particular clothes. It's purely and simply to impress other humans. They want the latest and most expensive clothing made out of the latest and most expensive materials. That's usually the last thing they need for good hunting, but then, that's often not their most important motive.

Well, enough about clothing. I'm going to the warm springs I have found on my ranch and soak my feet. I'll write again soon.

Love,

Buck

A Good Knife, Like a Good Friend

Deer Dad:

How is your health? Are you taking care of yourself? I know these are questions you used to ask me, but I guess now the tables are turned, and I do worry about you.

I also worry about some hunters. You know, Dad, there are all kinds of hunters doing all kinds of strange things. Some of them are generally good people, satisfying primitive urges beyond their control. They do come in all shapes and sizes with different degrees of ability and expertise. There is one thing that they all too often neglect that is really important to their success and well being. They will often underestimate the importance of a good knife. A good knife is more important than a good friend when hunters are out in the field. In fact, a good knife is a good friend, one that won't let the hunter down, as a "good friend" might.

Why is a good knife so important? It does so many things to help the hunter. Its main purpose is to cut. Cutting is often helpful and occasionally lifesaving. There is no way I can give you a complete list of everything a good knife can cut, but examples are string, cloth, food, and, of course, skin and other essential deer parts during the course of field dressing.

Selecting the proper knife again requires some decision making. Some knives fold in half and store the blade in the handle. Other knife blades are fixed. The former are safer when carried. The latter require a sheath to protect the blade from damage and humans from injury. Humans naturally develop a strong preference for one or another type, but, in fact, there is probably not much difference in performance.

The real quality of the knife is in the materials used in the construction, particularly the blade, and the workmanship in producing it, again particularly in the blade and especially in the cutting edge. It is most desirable to have a blade that has a good sharp edge and one that will retain that edge during normal use. Of course, humans do have a tendency to abuse their equipment. No knife normally available is designed to cut things such as metal, rock, bone, or other hard objects. A careless human can easily destroy the most expensive and highest quality knife by abuse.

Once purchased, the knife must also be cared for properly. It must be cleaned completely and as quickly as possible after it is used. It will rust if left wet, scratch if left dirty, and generally deteriorate unless kept clean and oiled.

When the cutting edge becomes dull, it needs to be sharpened. There are various devices available to do this successfully. Some depend upon a high level of skill. A simple whetstone is such a device. A knowledgeable human can use it to produce a perfect edge. An unskilled human can take an expensive knife and destroy it. There are sharpening tools that take the guesswork out of knife sharpening by mechanically creating the proper angle between the knife and the stone so that just about any human can do a creditable job.

So, Dad, the bottom line (as humans like to say) is to buy a high quality knife even if it is a bit more expensive and give it the love and care it deserves. It will pay dividends.

Love,

Buck

Miscellaneous Equipment

Deer Dad:

I've been writing to you about hunting preparations. Please remember we have to be continuously prepared for hunters. As you know, the smart hunter will prepare well for a hunting trip regardless of how long he plans to be in the field and away from home. That means appropriate selection of equipment. I'm not talking of things like weapons. I have written to you about them before. There are many other things that a smart hunter will bring along to make the trip successful. There are also many things he doesn't really need but often brings along out of ignorance or habit.

I really can't describe any of this equipment in much detail. I know you are not able to read for long periods of time, but I thought I would mention some of them briefly. Most of the items are self-explanatory and their use obvious, as long as the hunter remembers to pack them and use them during the hunt.

First of all, a flashlight is essential. I am not talking about a searchlight or spotlight for any of those illegal hunting schemes that unscrupulous humans use. I am talking about a small light that will easily fit into a pocket. If he is truly hunting, the human will want to start out well before sunrise and finish well after dark. A flashlight is very handy for getting into and out of blinds and the like when it is dark. Batteries always wear out when they are needed most, so an extra set would always be in order. Some flashlights are waterproof and even made to withstand being submerged. One of those would really be clever in the field.

Gloves are very important. They serve several essential functions. If it's cold, they will keep the hunter's hands warm. They will also serve as protection against all the possible things that can cause injury to the skin and other parts of human hands. Humans are constantly putting their appendages in the wrong places and gloves for the hands and boots for the feet are important for protection. Leather gloves are nice (animal products you know), and wool linings (more animals) are warm. It is wise, however, to make sure the gloves are not so large and cumbersome that they will interfere with the primary purpose of the hunt. If the fingers of the gloves are too big to fit into the trigger guard of the rifle, then only the deer will benefit.

There are a variety of items that I will just mention in passing. If it's really cold, humans can use artificial hand warmers in addition to gloves.

If there is going to be a great deal of shooting, then ear protectors may be helpful, although I don't understand why deer hunting should sound like a human war. Careful shooting should result in minimal shots, one bullet for each deer. In this case, quantity does not make up for quality.

In the area of hunter comfort, insect repellent is critical if the property contains such varmints as mosquitoes. In some parts of my territory, the mosquitoes dress out at three or four pounds. Some of them have landing lights.

Some contingency items would include a compass to use when the hunter gets lost and something to mark a trail so he doesn't. A first aid kit can forestall major injury and prolong time in the field instead of time in the hospital. Sunglasses will provide comfort during daytime hunting and those little packages that contain moist towelettes can be very refreshing in hot and dry areas.

Field dressing kits are a nice touch and very useful if the hunter gets lucky and shoots a deer. They usually contain plastic gloves to protect hands and forearms, a plastic bag for saving wanted internal organs, a plastic deer tag holder with a wire for attaching the tag to the deer, and some antiseptic skin ointment and band aids along with a moist towlette for cleaning after the "operation." Finally, the smart hunter should always have some lightweight but strong string. It will have a million uses.

Once the hunter gathers all of this in preparation for the hunt, it is a very good idea for him to keep it together as well. He should acquire a strong and roomy hunting bag to hold all of his equipment in one place, ready at all times to take with him, ensuring that he has not forgotten something vital.

Remember, Dad, hunters are likely to bring much more equipment than they need with them. Deer hunting is not like an African safari. Rarely is the hunter that far away from civilization, and many of the things he brings will just return home with him unused. The hunter should remember that if he didn't use it on an earlier hunt he should consider not bringing it again.

Enough for now. I will write again soon.

Love,

Buck

Equipment Care

Deer Dad:

I hope this letter finds you well. I'm really getting into the habit of writing these letters to you and I appreciate your interest in reading them. I know it's hard for you to write back so just send an occasional message with some friendly animal passing through and I will be happy.

I thought I would tell you about a human trait I have observed recently. I think it will interest you. I saw a few hunters the other day while they were having lunch. As I watched them from behind some brush, I saw them carelessly lay their rifles down in the dirt so they could eat and drink. They took virtually no care to see that these very expensive weapons were protected at all. I don't even think they realized what they were doing.

The point is that some humans really care very little for their possessions. It almost appears that their only desire is to acquire things, and, once they have them, their possessions are treated without regard. That's really a problem for hunters because if they don't maintain their hunting equipment properly the equipment will not function correctly when needed. If the equipment functions poorly that gives us a decided advantage; therefore, I'm not complaining. It's just a shame that all this fancy and expensive stuff gets mistreated and virtually destroyed. I guess we're really better off that we have no equipment to worry about. It makes our lives easier.

Interestingly, the hunting equipment humans need is quite easy to maintain and should not represent any great hardship. A little bit of time is not too much to spend for something so important.

What about rifles? The hunter should take precautions to protect the inner working mechanisms from dirt, water, and other foreign materials during the hunt. In addition to safety reasons, this kind of protection will make the rifle last longer and work better. It should be cleaned after use. There are inexpensive kits available with all the materials needed to do this, but, of course, the kit does no good if it remains on the shelf and never gets used. A rifle that is dirty won't shoot straight.

The telescopic sights on the rifle also need to be kept clean and dry. Hunters can purchase little plastic covers that will flip up and down to protect the lenses when they are not in use. The covers will really help protect the delicate lens mechanism and make the sights last longer.

Next to the rifle used by the hunter, the knife is most important. As I have written to you before, a good sharp knife is a great help in many ways, but it, too, must be kept clean and dry and oiled to protect it. In fact, a good rule of thumb for most everything I have mentioned as well as clothing and other hunting equipment is clean and dry. Yet it seems that everything about hunting is dirty and wet. The smart hunter will be constantly aware that Mother Nature will do everything to help destroy his equipment.

Say hello to Mother Nature for me when you see her, Dad.

Love,

Buck

To See is Not to Sight

Deer Dad:

You know that hunting season is rapidly approaching. It always brings back memories of past seasons to me as I prepare. Humans probably don't even realize that we deer also have to get ready for the season. Our preparations can be quite extensive. The interesting thing is that we have to do many of the same things humans have to do, or at least should do, if they want successful results from their efforts.

As I have written to you before, Dad, a successful hunt must include proper scouting of the wildlife population before the hunting season starts. Well, as you know, we have to do the same thing except in reverse. Once we determine where the hunters are spending their time scouting for us, we have to find suitable hiding places in some other part of the country. One of the reasons I like my present home is that the landowner will not allow too many hunters on the property and there is plenty of room for me to develop several good hiding places far away from where the humans will be hunting.

Fortunately, one of the things we do not have to worry about is preparing a weapon. I have written to you about the different types of rifles available and how humans have such problems deciding on the best weapon to use. Regardless of which weapon they do use, preparation of the weapon prior to the hunt is a critical step in the process.

Most important, if not key to the entire preparation process, is sighting in the rifle. It doesn't matter what brand of rifle or what sighting mechanism the hunter uses if he doesn't use accurate sights. Without accurate sights, even an expert hunter will act like a boob.

One of the biggest advantages we deer have in the struggle for survival with the humans is that they just don't realize the importance of this sighting in process. If they do understand why it should be done, few of them know how to do it properly.

Most of the time humans are so busy with their other activities that they just put off this process. Actually, most of them don't want to do it, and they find every possible excuse to delay. If they put it off long enough and wait until the last minute, then, with any luck, it will rain on the last possible day and the rationalization that they can always do it in camp will ensure that it never gets done at all.

Also, even if they do sight their weapon in carefully and accurately, with any luck the hunter will have to fly on a commercial airliner to get to the property and we can count on the baggage handlers to bounce the rifle around enough to knock it out of alignment. Unless the hunter is a true fanatic, he will not bother to sight in the rifle again and will explain away missed shots with some other excuse, and we can survive the entire season. On the other hand, with a good rifle, good sights, good gun case, and a fanatical human, we could be in real trouble.

Among the many subjects guaranteed to generate hours of human discussion is the correct way to sight in a rifle and where to set the pattern of shots. Of course, they could go on discussing the problem forever because there is no correct answer. It all depends! It all depends on where he is hunting, what the terrain is like, how thick the foliage is, and many other factors. So, it becomes essential to use different methods as needed.

First of all, the hunter needs to remember that even the same brand of commercially loaded bullets will vary slightly in their shooting characteristics because the loads will vary slightly. To ensure the most accuracy using commercially loaded shells, the hunter should verify they are all of the same brand, the same weight of load, and even all the same lot number, indicating that they were all loaded by the same machine at the same time. This means the hunter has to purchase enough shells at one time for the entire process. Shells aren't cheap and many hunters are, so this dictum isn't always followed. Of course, as I have written to you before, the true fanatic will load his own shells to maintain accuracy and reproducibility.

The best place to sight in a rifle is on a range where the distances are accurately measured and it's safe. There are a variety of commercially available targets that are inexpensive. A soft drink can does not qualify.

It is important for the hunter to shoot from a stable platform. Again, commercially available rests are available, as are sandbags and other types of support. The hunter needs to make sure he holds the rifle in a stable and safe position.

He should not be satisfied until he can fire a reproducible group of shots close together. A group has to have at least three in it and close may vary, but within an inch is nice. Reproducible means just that. He needs more than one to call it reproducible.

If he knows that he will never have a shot greater than one hundred yards, then he doesn't have to sight in the rifle for two hundred yards. On the other hand, long shots won't work with a rifle sighted in on the bull's-eye for fifty yards. The shots in the field will be low.

Once again, he has to know his hunting site geography and plan accordingly. Many experts feel it is appropriate to sight every rifle a bit high to account for the ballistic characteristics of the caliber of the ammunition. Most manufacturers will describe these characteristics either on the box of shells or in accompanying literature so that the hunter can determine how flat or curved the trajectory is for that caliber. It really is a complicated business. Once again, there are many experts. Unfortunately, there are also many people who call themselves experts who really are not. The intelligent neophyte should find a successful hunter and discuss it with him. Hopefully, it will not be an endless discussion and he can gain some good tips on how to do the job correctly.

I'm sorry this letter is so long. Take care of yourself.

Love,

Buck

Opening Day

Deer Dad:

Don't worry! Everything here is fine. I sent this letter via express mail so you would get it quickly. Tomorrow is "opening day," and I wanted to make sure you got this letter before sunrise. I know the pressure everyone is under, especially the mail service.

I've been listening to the hunters on my ranch talking again. Actually, I should say arguing again. They argue about the strangest topics. Today they were discussing the best time to hunt. Oh, I don't mean time of day (I will write a letter about that later); I mean the best time during the season.

They make everything sound so complicated. One human spent over an hour trying to convince the others that opening day and/or as early as possible in the season is the best time to hunt and is far superior to all other times. There is some merit to this point of view; however, a true hunter feels the best time of the season to hunt is all season.

The decision to hunt early in the season is usually based on the concept that we are not ready for hunting on opening day because it's been so long since anyone hunted us. The issue in question is does a deer remember. Imagine that, they think we have no capacity for memory.

One of the big problems with humans is that they under estimate all other creatures. They credit only themselves with any capacities such as memory, logic, mathematical aptitude, or other capabilities. It's not so strange that they feel this way about us "lower forms of life." They even feel that way about each other.

Can you imagine that some groups of humans actually feel that other groups of humans are inferior? They make these decisions based on a variety of factors such as race, religion, country of origin, and, in some cases, college attended.

There is an entire category of human humor called ethnic jokes. One group makes fun of another group in the name of humor. They have made particular fun of Polish people and a group called

Aggies. I'm not sure what an Aggie is, much less why they deserve to be the butt of this type of humor. The funny thing is, the more humans are made fun of, the better they seem to like it. They actually thrive on this type of attention. It makes them stand together in the face of adversity, and, in standing together they derive strength from each other.

Where was I? Oh, yes I was writing about the question of deer memory. How could we forget last hunting season? We spent several months watching these humans cavorting about the countryside literally making fools of themselves. They shot at cows, barns, other humans, and, occasionally, deer. They made noise and actually seemed to be enjoying themselves. You and I know we haven't forgotten. We have spent the off-season being careful and preparing for this new season. We are ready. We will not be caught napping. We have reconditioned our old homes and developed new places to hide when the pressure gets tough.

Still, those hunters that do start early in the season will have a good experience if they follow all the other rules of good hunting practices. They have chosen a good area in which to hunt, they have scouted the area well, and they have taken the trouble to prepare their equipment and their minds for the hunting season.

The most important advantage they will have in early season hunting is that they will get the "jump" on many of their companions. The trouble is that many of these humans who think early hunting is best will be out on opening day. The number of hunters will be huge. Those that hunt on property that does not correctly limit the number of hunters are at serious risk for their own safety. They had better be careful.

There are other times to hunt besides opening day or very early in the season. I will write to you about some advantages and disadvantages in future letters.

For now, take care of yourself. Remember that even though I know we have good memory processes, as we get older they do diminish. Humans have the same problem. In fact, they have a name for the disease that affects their memory as they get older, but I can't remember what they call it right now. Anyway, don't forget that we can forget.

Love,

Buck

Mid-Season Special

Deer Dad:

I hope you are well and I hope you received my last letter. Opening day has come and gone. We survived another one. I have written you detailing the arguments hunters have with each other about the best time of the season to hunt. There are proponents of early season hunting, mid-season hunting, and late season hunting. Naturally, if they can't hunt all season, and their time is limited, then they have to determine the best time to hunt. There are advantages and disadvantages to each.

Mid-season hunting has some advantages that neither early or late season enjoy. It really has to do with something called human nature. Humans get all emotionally charged for hunting season. They spend all their time in the off-season dreaming about the deer that got away and how they are not going to let that happen next season. Of course, their big problem is all they do is dream; they do precious little to prepare not to let it happen again. That's one for our side.

Anyway, they get all charged up just before the season. They scurry about trying to get ready, always giving themselves too little time to do the job right. Then, all of them try to go out opening day (I wrote you about this in the last letter). Because of human nature, after they make a big start they fade out and take it easy. I guess they figure there is still plenty of time and they get their priorities confused.

They get very confused, for example, with this thing they call football. Apparently it is a sport just like hunting. There the similarity ends. Hunting is an individual sport in which the human must participate. Football is a group activity in which the human can sit there, yell a bit, drink some, and then fight with his friends about the outcome of the game. Football is played on the weekends, just when a human does not have to work and when he could most easily go hunting. Often, football wins the priority struggle in the human's mind over hunting and he goes to the game or, worse, stays home and watches it on television. That means there are far fewer hunters in the field after the initial surge of opening weekend. Those that do set their priorities correctly and go hunting find that there are fewer hunters to worry about and they can concentrate more on the object of the activity, the deer.

Now the big disadvantage to mid-season hunting is that we deer have already been exposed to significant hunting pressure due to the surge of activity early in the season and have taken evasive action, moving into new and harder to find refuge. We make sure we move about less during the day and confine our activities to night. We will be harder to find. All this is assuming that the rut is not in progress. I will write about the rut later on, but you must remember that all rules the deer follow religiously the rest of the year are suspended during the rut.

It is essential for the hunter to appreciate when the rut starts and is in progress so that he can include this essential information in his hunting plans. It is possible to tell when the rut starts if the hunter is willing to do a little work and spend some time observing his surroundings. That information is so important I will discuss it in detail in a separate letter.

The rut aside, mid-season hunting can be very rewarding. I do suspect the decision to hunt versus watching a football game largely depends upon the quality of the hunting and certainly the quality of the football, although it's interesting that some of the worst football teams have the best attendance. This is especially true in the college games where more than the quality of the football sets the priorities. There is this status called "college alumni" that plays a major role in the hunter's decision making process. Having attended a college, even many years ago, seems to leave such a lasting impression on the human that he will often go through extreme hardships to attend a game at his alma mater. Hardships such as great distances, poor teams, expensive tickets, lousy food, and flat beer do nothing to dissuade him from his activity. Imagine all that and still he doesn't choose to go hunting.

In my next letter I will write about late season hunting. Then, after that, I will write about the rut, one of my favorite subjects.

Love,

Buck

Last Chance

Deer Dad:

The season is almost over. I hope you are well and safe. I told you I would write you about late season hunting, so here it is. Late season hunting often takes on an air of desperation. The hunter has spent varying amounts of time hunting up to that point and suddenly realizes that time is running out. He probably has seen some average bucks during his early season hunts but refrained from shooting any in search of the trophy he knows is just behind the next tree. Now, not only is the superior intelligence of the deer against him, so is time.

Situations such as this will produce things called ulcers in a human just as easily as losing his business, wife, girlfriend, or all three do. Should he settle for less than the best? That reminds me of the country and western song titled, "The girls always look prettier at closing time." Should he use the "I only hunt for meat" ploy? Should he petition the government for a delay to the end of the season? You see, he is in deep trouble.

What he really needs to do is plan for this in advance. He knows how many deer he is entitled to shoot during the season. Just as the astronaut scooped up some moon rocks as soon as he landed, the so-called "contingency specimens," so should the hunter plan his hunting season. He should time the shooting of the deer he feels he can accept, leaving one tag for the trophy he is likely to see on the last day. Of course, there is nothing wrong with not using all the tags he has, and, there is always next year!

There is a myth circulating that late season hunting will fool the deer who think that the season is over after Christmas. Not true. We know very well when the season is over, just as we know when it starts. We know when it's safe to show ourselves, so that the human can see what he missed and can whet his appetite for next year.

The secret to late season hunting is the same as the secret a football team has to use when its initial strategy doesn't seem to be working and the other team starts to pull ahead. The tendency for the losing coach is to change the game plan and start to use wild tactics to try to catch up. Instead, he should force himself and his team to do just the opposite and stick with the game plan and try to make it work.

Hunters do the same thing as losing coaches. They panic. Panic never works. Only planning works, and providing he planned well, knows where he is hunting, and remembers the characteristics of the deer activity, the hunter has the best chance of success.

Remember that we deer also have a game plan, and we are much less likely to vary from the game plan. We will continue our activities taking the same routes, using the same feeding and resting areas as we usually do, unless humans come around and disturb us. The hunter should keep to what he knows has worked in the past. If he runs us out in panic, there is no telling where we will go or what we will do and then all his plans are for nothing.

Finally, the hunter should remember that old expression that was coined by one of our deer ancestors. "The hunting isn't over until the fat lady sings." Loosely translated, that means he has up until the last minute of the last day to find and shoot his trophy. He should not quit early.

I still want to write about the rut and how that has to be calculated into the hunting equation each season. I will do that in a future letter.

Love,

Buck

Out of Season Bargains

Deer Dad:

I've written to you about the various times in the season to hunt including early, middle, and late season hunting. There is one more time to hunt that I think I should mention since it is very important to both of us. That is out of season hunting.

Very important human officials, called politicians, listened to other humans interested in game management when establishing certain times of the year during which hunting would be allowed. There are many important reasons that hunting seasons have been established but none more important than the control these seasons exert on preserving appropriate wildlife quality and numbers. The humans establish the length of the seasons, their timing during the year, and even the numbers and types of animals that can be hunted. If they continue to manage these things carefully, I am confident that deer, as a species, will survive many more centuries. Of course, if they get careless we are all in trouble.

Hunting at times other than during the established season is illegal. Remember that humans are strange animals. They will often do things that are illegal. The funny thing is that they usually know it's illegal but that doesn't seem to stop them. In fact, illegal activity is very important to the economy of the humans. If there were no illegal activity, there would be little need for large numbers of jobs and professions that humans need to maintain their economy. I need only mention such professions as lawyers and judges. Just think how few would be needed if there were no illegal activities. Then think of all the policemen, not to mention large industries such as jails and prisons, including the correctional officers, wardens, secretaries, and many, many, more, that would be superfluous. In fact, the financial impact of illegal activities probably represents the fastest growing sector of today's economy. It's mind boggling. Such an important industry will not disappear overnight no matter how clever the human politicians are who claim to have answers for all the social problems. In fact, just the opposite is true. The more questions they answer, the more new questions are raised, or, put another way, the solution to every problem creates several new problems.

What all this means to you and me is that out of season hunting will continue. Let me make it perfectly clear that out of season means not only before and after the regular dates set by the local authorities, but also hunting done during illegal times of day during the hunting season—particularly at night.

Because legal hunting is expensive and often difficult to arrange, many individuals resort to these illegal activities. They have no choice. I told you that there are very primitive urges in humans that go back to their caveman ancestors. These urges force them to commit illegal activities.

Here, Dad, I must insert a disclaimer. If a human should find this letter, I would not want them to use this "urge" business to justify his illegal activity, especially in his defense during criminal proceedings. I will not testify in court on this matter.

There are also other primitive urges that force humans to be territorial animals and to protect their territory. Through the ages they have done so with a vengeance. Look at all the human wars that have been fought over territorial disputes. Look at what used to happen to cattle rustlers or horse thieves in the old days. Well, the same is true currently when protecting property. Humans still have a long way to go to develop adequate laws and penalties to punish those who participate in illegal hunting, but they are getting better.

So, Dad, the answer to humans about out of season hunting is DON'T, DON'T, DON'T! I hope that all humans who can read will read this and heed my advice. I hope those that don't listen will be adequately punished.

Speaking of illegal activities, even those humans that hunt during appropriate times may do it illegally. I will write more about that in a future letter.

Love,

Buck

Beauty is in the Eye of the Beholder

Deer Dad:

The hunting season is over for another year. I know you survived and I hope you are well. It is fun to think back over the past few months and reminisce.

The closer the start of the deer hunting season, the closer human hunters get to overt mental illness. They begin to spend more and more time daydreaming about the hunt and less and less worrying about such things as the stock market and their jobs. They get that glazed-over look in the eyes as they plan and replan the mental image of finding, tracking, and shooting that trophy buck.

I wish I could actually look into their minds and see what their imaginary trophy buck looks like. I suppose no two would look alike. Every hunter has his own image and he constantly compares every buck he sees to that image. It absolutely guarantees that any buck shot by any other hunter is not the trophy buck he imagines. In fact, most of the other bucks he has seen are grossly inferior to his conjured trophy.

Well, if a neophyte hunter has yet to develop such a mental picture of what his ideal trophy should look like, perhaps I could enlighten him a bit by telling him what he should be looking for.

First of all, he will have some simple decisions to make. Trophy bucks come in two main varieties and, in fact, two categories in the Boone and Crockett Record Book. The ideal trophy must qualify as either a "typical" or "atypical" buck. Typical bucks have antler development that is symmetrical and regular with all tines pointing upward. Atypical bucks have antler development that does not assume this pattern and may have any bizarre appearance. Most often, dropped tines, pointing downward, are seen.

Either way, there are some characteristics that identify a buck as having superior quality in antler development. As you know, the Boone and Crockett Club keeps track of record bucks and awards points for a variety of measurements of antler growth. To score a rack accurately takes many measurements and is clearly not something that can be done by the hunter in the field when he is trying to decide whether or not to shoot a particular animal. When he has his binoculars on a buck he can still judge the thickness of the horns, the spread of the horns in their greatest diameter, and make some evaluation of the number and length of the tines. As a general rule, bigger, heavier, and more is better.

Symmetry is important but difficult to evaluate in the field. Thickness of the antlers particularly at the bases, number of brow tines, and the spatial relationships of the rack is also difficult to evaluate. If the horns spread outside the ears it is a good bet that the rack is worth considering.

Unfortunately for the hunter, what usually happens is that all he gets is a fleeting glimpse of the deer as he passes some open spot and the hunter hasn't got time to accurately assess the quality of the rack. He is faced with a split-second decision, and the natural tendency is to take what he can get and then worry later about the excuse he will need to explain why he shot such an inferior animal.

It is difficult to develop a mental attitude that he is going to wait for the trophy even if it means not shooting anything. That requires a certain hunting maturity that is beyond the capability of most hunters. Thank God!

I'll write you again soon.

Love,

Buck

Home Sweet Home

Deer Dad:

I was thinking about you today so I thought I'd drop you a line. Actually, I was feeling a bit homesick. You know, humans get homesick. That's why they write songs like "I'm going home for Christmas" and make samplers that say "Home, sweet, home" to hang on the wall. Well, we deer get homesick, too.

There are many myths about deer that humans believe. Usually, they don't apply at all and are just old wives' tales. A large number of humans think deer move around often and even migrate. Well, other species do migrate. Whales and geese are two examples. I really can't say about our cousins the reindeer. Those guys may do just about anything. They even let humans ride on top of them; whitetail deer definitely do not.

In fact, we stay close to home when we can. I would much prefer to live my whole life in the same neighborhood. I would be very happy to remain in an area of not more than a few hundred yards. After all, I am comfortable here. I have learned to satisfy all my needs here. I have several places to sleep. I have enough food and water. I even have enough female companionship when I want it. Also, the other bucks have learned that this is my home and usually they don't bother me. If they do come around to stick their noses into my business, I usually have little trouble convincing them to get out.

Oh, don't get me wrong! I will move if I have to. If the humans get too close to my territory, either because of hunting pressure or urbanization and excess human activity, I will move. I will find a new home suitable to my needs, but I would just rather not.

This fact is important to those hunters who pay attention to the deer in order to learn from us. They are the intelligent hunters. There are some of them around. They keep their eyes and ears open and learn from what they observe. Experienced hunters will confirm that they see the same animals in the same places year after year. We may have slight differences in the configuration of our antlers from year to year, but our overall general appearance will remain the same and we can be identified. It's odd how every species and even groups within the species have little trouble identifying individuals within the group but often tell you that they can't tell the differences in other groups—that "they all look alike."

Anyway, I like to stay home. I even miss my former home with you. Of course, when I got old enough I had to move away from you, just as my kids have had to do the same, but I want you to know that I miss you. I'll bet humans don't believe that we deer can have emotions.

We can also experience a feeling called ambivalence. At least I do, that's why I have written to you about appropriate game management techniques even though I know that if humans follow the measures I described it will result in some of our species being destroyed. I know that overall we will benefit from sound game management practices and our species will be better off. What really makes me sad is the thought that humans are very hardheaded. Many landowners will not even listen to their own experts, much less me, about these scientifically demonstrated concepts and their value. I think that's called human nature.

Love,

Buck

Rainy Day Activities

Deer Dad:

I hope you are well. Everything is really great here. It's rainy, foggy, and getting colder. Of course, that makes it even better. You know, Dad, that's one thing humans don't understand. When they hunt they want the weather to be warm, clear, and sunny. The trouble is they want that for the wrong reason. They like "nice" weather for their own comfort. What they should want is the best weather for hunting.

Good weather from the deer's point of view is as it is today. Fog is really the best for us. Hunters just can't see us in the fog. Rain doesn't bother us, of course. We have nice, well-insulated hides to protect us. Humans, unfortunately, have something they call skin, and it is very thin at best. Of course, they do wear cumbersome clothing over their skin, but all that does is inhibit free and easy movement. So, hunters don't like rain any more than they like fog.

The same can be said for cold. Hunters don't like it much because they have to wear heavy clothing to keep warm. We love cold weather, not only because it inconveniences hunters, but because somehow it is associated with the rutting season. You know what that means! (You do remember, don't you?)

Hunters spend time trying to figure out when we move about assuming that they have a better chance to find us when we are moving. Well, that is true. You know very well that there are a million places even a half-smart deer can find to bed down that even the most expert hunter could never find. In fact, I spend a great deal of time each year identifying several hiding places so that I can have appropriate alternatives should the need arise.

Unfortunately, we do have to eat and drink so we can't stay in a secure place the entire hunting season and thereby stay away from hunters. In that regard, our friends the bears have a pretty good deal. They can hibernate the winter away in the safety of some secure cave and never get involved with humans at all. Some day I may try to find out why and how they do that and see if I can't make a major impact on the sport of deer hunting.

Be that as it may, we have to get up a few times a day and get out to sustain ourselves. The best time to do it is at night. Without using illegal means, humans can't get to us at night. If we can't eat at night, then early in the morning or late evening is certainly better then in broad daylight. Since most hunters don't like to get up early, we have a much better chance of survival if we start and finish our forays before the humans get to their respective hunting spots. Then they can look all day, not find us, blame it on some unrelated event, and go back home with some camphouse stories and not much else.

By the way, the excuses hunters have for not finding deer, missing shots, and explaining everything else that can go wrong would fill a book. I will tell you about some of them in future letters.

The fog is beginning to lift and the rain is letting up. I think I'll go back deeper into the brush in case any humans get brave enough to combat the elements and come looking.

Love,

Buck

The Lay of the Land

Deer Dad:

As soon as I mailed the last letter to you, the weather turned cold and it snowed. I didn't like it. I know our relatives up north think snow is great. I could see my tracks and I'm sure so could a human.

In my last letter we talked about how important the weather is in successful (or unsuccessful, depending on your point of view) deer hunting. You realize that weather is only one small part of the whole picture. Another very important feature is terrain. What I mean is the "lay of the land," so to speak. Most human hunters would prefer to sit up in some high (and dry) blind in the center of a perfectly flat pasture seven or eight hundred years in diameter, without any obstructions, and have a steady parade of trophy bucks pass in front of them. That may happen in fantasy land, but it's not going to happen in the real world.

If a landowner sets up such a situation and then tries to sell a lease, the hunter should beware. We deer do not frequent flat open pastures. In fact, we like just the opposite. We like places to hide. We are, by our very nature, shy and suspicious animals. Hunters should notice how we cross the road. In fact, Dad, did you know that the old human adage taught to every school child, "Look both ways before you cross," came from us deer? I know humans have taught their children to cross the street this way. Well, it's the same way we cross. We stay concealed behind some shrubs or something and look all ways before we cross, listening for foreign noises and unusual smells. I will admit that during times of imminent danger we may just run across as rapidly as possible, but it's not likely that a hunter will ever hit a deer who is running "flat out" anyway. When we perceive no danger, we will make darn sure there is no enemy waiting for us to cross the road.

We like ravines, gullies, and all sorts of hiding places. The more there are, the more likely we will adopt such a place in which to live. Trees are nice, as is heavy brush. We want cover. If a rancher wants deer on his property, he should make sure this type of habitat is available. Of course, we want this habitat for food, but don't get me wrong. Even if he were to provide mountains of corn, oats, and everything else we like, without protective cover we would not even look at the place, much less sign a long term lease.

Well, we don't actually sign leases like humans, but we do maintain a remarkable stability in our home range. Unless we encounter some long term problem such as no food, no water, or the presence of a new shopping center, most of us will reside in the same general vicinity all our lives.

If hunters want to be successful, they should pay considerable attention to the terrain of the place they propose to hunt. It is essential to select the proper terrain and also important to understand the fine nuances of the selected geography. I have seen hunters set up shop in a poorly selected spot and be unsuccessful, when moving only small distances would have afforded them the best hunting of their lives.

Success in hunting depends on scouting. Scouting correctly is a complicated process with many factors. I will probably spend a whole letter about scouting.

Dad, take care of yourself. I know that you are getting restless and worried about your health. Just remember to eat well and get some exercise—but do it at night, please.

Love,

Buck

To Scout or Not to Scout

Deer Dad:

I hope this letter finds you well. Actually, I hope this letter finds you. It occurs to me, Dad, that I have written to you often in the last few months and I have heard precious little from you. Actually, I realize that it is very difficult for you to write, and I did appreciate the message you sent with that black buck antelope that was passing through. I do hope that you are reading these notes and keeping them in a safe place. As you know, I do have it in the back of my mind to consider publishing them in the form of a book someday. I first have to decide if humans would find them interesting enough to pay money for them. Then, of course, I would have to decide how to spend the money I earned from the royalties. I think I would probably invest the money and use the interest to further education and gun safety for hunters. Some hunters are outright dangerous and others could really use some straightforward learning about deer hunting. I think intelligent hunters would only contribute to the overall quality of the deer population in this country.

Anyway, I want to write you a little about scouting. I know I have mentioned this in previous letters, but I don't think I have stressed the importance of this practice enough. In fact, I don't think I could ever stress it too much, it is so important to hunting success.

Actually, scouting is a year-round activity. It should begin as soon as the hunting season is completed and should continue all year long.

Impossible, you say? Humans have to do other things besides walk or ride around a ranch all day looking for deer. Not the smart ones! I know that there are some other activities that require human's attention, but that doesn't change the story. The more time a hunter spends observing the wildlife on a piece of property, the more time he spends learning as much about the topography as possible, the better chance he will have of finding and shooting a trophy buck next season.

The hunter who requires a lease on which to hunt because he was not smart enough to be born into one should consider the distance the lease is located from his home and should make sure that the landowner will allow him access to the property during the off season so that he can spend as much time as possible scouting.

One alternative, not as good as scouting the property himself, is to have someone else do it for him. If he is a guest invited to hunt, his host will usually be able to help him choose good hunting spots. If he has a good friend with some spare time, he may be able to impose on the friend to scout for him. He better be careful, though. He had better choose a good friend and preferably not one who shares the lease, or the friend may just take it into his head to pass along some false information and keep the good scouting findings for himself. Not his friend, you say? Ho, Ho, Ho, I say, and I'm not Santa Claus.

In summary, the more the hunter scouts, the better success he will have. Maybe he won't have to say, "Wait until next season".

Love,

Buck

Time of Day

Deer Dad:

I have sent you several letters dealing with the decisions humans have to make about the best time in the season to hunt. You remember, from their point of view we decided that any time is the best time to hunt, barring any roadblocks like wives and football games.

There is another question that humans often have difficulty answering clearly. That is when during the day is the best time to hunt. Given the fact that night hunting is a NO NO, there is still plenty of daylight for the hunter to get out and get busy. Is there one best time (again, besides all the time)?

As you'd expect, there are experts that will swear there is one best time of the day and all the other times are worthless. There are proponents for early morning, late evening, noon, and just about every time in between.

It makes sense, to a simple deer like me, that the more time spent in the field, the better chance of seeing and shooting one of us. It has not been my experience that deer frequent the inside of camphouses—not live deer anyway. Some do come very close to these dens of iniquity, for educational purposes, but it's not likely we will enter one of these places, tiptoe over to a sleeping hunter, wake him gently, give him his rifle, and then let him get a good shot at us. No, unfortunately, even in the most ideal hunting circumstances the hunter is going to have to go outside and get a bit dirty in the process.

From the hunter's point of view, early morning is good. If he gets out early enough, he may find some of us on our morning rounds or returning from our evening activities.

Remember, Dad, I said early. A hunter has to be out to his chosen hunting site well before sunrise. He has to be settled in, quiet, and hidden before daylight. Fooling around in the camphouse, having a second cup of coffee, then climbing into a noisy vehicle for a loud ride to where he is going—having all this activity occur during daylight and still expect us to ignore all this—is asking too much of

91

our superior intellect. Even a human wouldn't fall for that. Early is the key.

The same rule applies for evening hunting. To see deer in the late afternoon, the hunter has to get out several hours before dusk to let the intrusion he has made settle down before we deer will think things are back to normal and resume our activities.

There is also a notion around that deer never move about during the day, that we find a place to hide and stay there all during the daylight hours. Unfortunately, this is not always true. If we were smart, we would follow this advice, but, just as with humans, there are all kinds of deer. Some of us just want exercise, others get scared and move when they sense danger and don't think they are safe where they are hiding.

The bottom line is that deer move all day and while there may be more activity early and late in the day, if the hunter needs a deer he better get out and find one. He should stay out all day and make the most of the environment. Even if he doesn't see many deer, he will be amazed at what he will see. It's worth it. We deer do it all the time.

Take care of yourself, Dad, and remember to stay put during the day, if you can.

Love,

Buck

Blinds and Blinds

Deer Dad:

Summer is almost over here. The water is plentiful and my landowner has planted some lovely oats for me to eat.

I promised to write more to you about the preparations my landowner is making for the upcoming season. I know it's getting closer because of the frenzy around the place.

In this letter I thought I'd tell you about the blinds that he is setting up. Blinds are places for hunters to sit and try to hide so that they can shoot us as we pass. Inherent in the concept of a successful blind is that it will be in a place where we frequent. It would really be dumb to set up a blind in a spot where we never go. Sometimes, humans are really dumb.

First, therefore, the hunter has to determine where we walk, or he can try to be clever and set one up where he wants us to walk and then develop some strategy to get us there.

He can remember where we walked last year. He knows we are creatures of habit and will usually use the same trails we have used in the past. He can scout the territory looking for us well before the season starts, knowing we will probably maintain our movement patterns. Even if he doesn't see us he can see our trails in the dirt, fresh droppings, and so forth, and know we have been in the area. He can also set up feeders, oat fields, ponds of water, and other enticements to get us to go where he wants.

He has to keep safety in mind. It would be inappropriate to set up two blinds in such a way that a hunter sitting in one could even potentially shoot at a hunter in another should a deer walk between them.

Once he selects a likely site for the blind, he must be sure that when the blind is erected the hunter will have clear views from which to shoot. The line of sight should be unobstructed as much as possible and still maintain the camouflaged nature of the blind. The best way to make a hunter unhappy is to allow him to see a trophy buck but be unable to get a shot at him because there was a big bush or tree directly in his line of fire.

Dad, as you know, there are all types of blinds. There are blinds made of natural materials found in and around the area of the intended blind. There are completely manufactured blinds that can be erected on the site. There are ground blinds and elevated blinds, hidden blinds and open blinds.

Once a location that seems suitable is identified, a careful survey of the topography in the area is important. Are there any natural elevations, projections, or any other areas that already exist to preclude the need to make an artificial blind?

A blind can be set up facing any direction, but in setting up a blind such considerations as the direction of the sun during the day, wind direction versus expected deer movement, etc., must be evaluated. Since the purpose of a natural blind is to blend in with the surroundings, once the decision is made that the site is appropriate, the hunter should carefully select materials to be used. If minimal shifting of already existing materials will work, that is the best. Perhaps he can rearrange a fallen tree or some bushes already at the site.

If the hunter plans to erect an artificial blind, then he must make other decisions. How portable does he want the blind? Will it be advantageous to have the blind and hunter completely hidden, or is it all right to be out in the open? How important is it that the hunter be able to get into and out of the blind easily? Obviously, in order to answer the last question, some knowledge of who will be using the blind is important.

The two most common artificial blinds are chair blinds and enclosed structures. Chair blinds, usually elevated on a tripod, are completely open and offer no protection from the elements. They rotate 360 degrees and usually have a rest from which to shoot. Of course, they must be placed so that they are hidden from the spots most likely to contain deer, yet still offer a clear shot.

Some hunters like to get up high. They will even climb a tree to get a good view of the landscape. I know what you are thinking and I agree with you, Dad, it's rather awkward to me. Humans can purchase a metal contraption that goes around a tree and creates a little platform to sit or stand on, but it's still a strange way to find a deer.

Enclosed blinds vary from simple wooden boxes to very elaborate structures resembling homes. They all should have a few characteristics in common. They should have a reasonably easy entry for the hunter. They should have visibility from all sides and a suitable rest from which to shoot. After that, all bets are off. Believe it or not, Dad, some blinds are heated, air-conditioned, carpeted, have running water, bathrooms, radio, and television. Some hunters do strange things in blinds besides hunt. I have it on very good authority that human couples have been known to perform their own version of the rut in these structures. Amazing!

Nevertheless, if the landowner and hunter desire success in blind use, then they must carefully place the correct blind. Oh, by the way, humans think we cannot hear or see. Naturally, we can do both, although we are color blind. We can hear even the tiniest sounds and see even the slightest movement. Humans also forget we can smell. We do that best of all. It does no good to set up a beautiful blind and then disregard these factors when using it.

All of this writing has made me hungry. It's dark enough to go find some food. I'll write again soon.

Love,

Buck

The Purist

Deer Dad:

I hope you are well. I have been worried about you lately with all these hunters running around. Some may get lucky.

I have written to you recently about blinds and feeders. Both of these human inventions are designed to improve the edge humans think they need over us during the hunt. Apparently, they feel the odds are not strong enough in their favor and they have developed these techniques to even the score.

I must tell you that there are some humans who don't believe in such practices. There are some who actually feel that hunting is a sport and that the game should be given an even chance. As I have mentioned before, winning has an entirely different connotation to a human than winning has to us. If he loses, he goes home. If we lose, we go to the big pasture in the sky.

Nevertheless, I, for one, must think kindly of the hunting purist. I favor his techniques. He does not use such human contraptions as blinds or feeders. Instead, he prefers to meet the deer on the deer's terms in the field. He believes that using a technique called "still hunting" is the most enjoyable for him and most fair for the deer. So it is.

If he is a complete purist he will not even use a rifle; rather, he will use a more equitable weapon like a bow and arrow. Of course, this requires much more skill, not only in shooting the weapon but also in getting the close range required to shoot accurately and with sufficient force to be effective.

Weapons aside, "still hunting" requires much more skill and self-dicipline than other types of hunting. Success, however, has a much better taste. "Still hunting" actually means getting out and walking, tracking, and stalking the deer. The hunter will have to search for signs that deer have been in the area. He will have to recognize deer tracks, fresh deer droppings, scrapes during the rut, deer rubbings on low trees and bushes, and even, when he becomes sophisticated, deer scent.

When I say walking, I don't really mean walking either. I really mean very slow, quiet moving, studying the terrain very carefully, and barely proceeding in any given direction. By starting off in an area known to contain deer and moving at a barely perceptible speed, it is possible for the hunter to see a deer before the deer sees him and keeping him unaware of his presence, actually move quite close. As I mentioned, the hunter must keep all of the factors such as wind direction, elevation, noise, and so forth constantly in mind and move extremely cautiously or the hunt will be over before it starts and the deer will disappear.

If the neophyte "still hunter" foolishly keeps upwind of the deer, he will return to the camphouse with a story that no deer were present. If, on the other hand, he is able to keep all the factors that play a role in "still hunting" in mind and is successful in carrying them out, then he will be able to tell stories about deer activity that would hardly be believed. "Still hunting" has much to commend it. It is the most challenging type of hunting and certainly should be tried by all hunters once they feel confident that they understand the principles involved.

Take care of yourself and remember to stay downwind of all humans.

Love,

Buck

The Rut

Deer Dad:

Please excuse the delay in this letter. I know I promised to write you sooner, but I have been trying to compose my thoughts about the rut for some time now and I am finding it difficult to get everything down the way I want. You know the rut is a special time for us deer. In fact, were it not a special time for you, I would not have been here to write this letter.

Without the rut we would have become extinct long ago. It's a time of spurting hormones and surging passion. I don't want to bore you with the physiology of the rut, although entire books have been written on the subject and they make for quite interesting reading. Humans have spent countless hours and dollars investigating the details of the rut in an attempt to learn what starts it and exactly what happens to us during this crucial time period.

All I know is, although it is essential to survival of our species, it puts us at extreme risk, because it usually occurs during hunting season. While we are generally cautious and clever about our dealings with humans, during the rut all bets are off and we do crazy things we would never do normally. These activities, if properly understood and capitalized upon by all hunters, would be worse for us than no rut at all.

Dad, don't get me wrong. I look forward to the rut each year. I want my share of the activities. As careful as I am, even I realize that I do stupid things in the name of love (or at least in the name of lust). I fear that when my time comes it will be during the rut, when I least expect it. Unfortunately, when I least expect it is probably when I am enjoying the rut the most.

I once saw a most unusual circumstance that ended in the unfortunate death of a fine buck but demonstrated that not all humans are the heartless creatures some would have you believe. I witnessed a group of hunters in a pickup truck suddenly come upon this buck and a comely doe in the middle of a sexual experience. The hunters stopped the truck and had ample opportunity to shoot both the buck and doe several times over if they had so desired, so oblivious were both deer to their imminent danger. Nevertheless, the hunters did not interrupt the deer; rather, they calmly waited until the deer were finished and had separated. Then, of course, one of them shot the buck and ended his career. Still, they had been gentlemen enough to allow the buck his last bit of fun. In fact, the buck was a trophy caliber and I heard them say that the hunter planned to mount the deer with a cigarette in his mouth, whatever that means.

You see, Dad, even though I tried to take my time and compose this letter carefully, I have already strayed considerably from the point. The rut changes everything when it comes to planning a deer hunt because we deer will do such uncharacteristic things that a smart human will capitalize on our emotions.

For example, you know we would try to avoid moving about during the day any other time of the year, lest we meet a hunter or some other enemy and not be prepared to deal with the situation. During the rut, we disregard this procedure and keep moving about making scrapes (I'll write more about scrapes and such in a future letter), identifying our territory, and issuing invitations to ladies to join us for a bit of excitement. When we do this, we usually become oblivious to outside danger. We are vulnerable. If a hunter learns how to recognize a scrape, he can identify the rut, and by estimating how fresh the scrape is he can tell our movement.

Also, our attention switches from worrying about hunters to worrying about other bucks during the rut. We are very territorial animals and would take great offense if some other buck thought about invading our territory just when we plan to mate with a doe. More than one fight to the death has occurred between two bucks during this time. We are attracted to other bucks fighting by the noise their antlers make when they strike each other during the fight. A clever human, simulating the sound of antlers banging together (so-called rattling, about which I'll write more later), could easily fool us into investigating the noise and being shot for our trouble. We would never do this during the rest of the year, but during the rut we tend to lose all our caution, and we seem to be controlled by our testosterone rather than by our brain.

What I'm trying to say is that if a hunter is smart, he will determine when the rut will take place, or at least, when the rut has started so he can hunt during that time. The timing of the rut varies depending upon the location of the property. There is some relationship to weather, temperature, and length of daylight hours so that the rut starts much earlier in the northern states than it does down south. With any luck for the hunter, the rut will occur during some part of his hunting activities.

Identifying the rut and its associated activities and the details of rattling and so forth will be the subjects of future letters. I will share with you some of the things I have learned about good hunting tactics.

Love,

Buck

Rattling and Other Kid Games

Deer Dad:

I thought I'd drop you a note and tell you how I am doing. To tell you the truth, I'm getting those funny feelings again that tell me the rut is beginning. You know how strange things become for us deer during this time of year. Just when we should be the most careful, we get the most reckless. We seem to do everything we can to give the hunters extra advantages. God knows they don't need any more advantages then they already have. They have those rifles with telescopic sights, blinds, feeders, radar, and sonar.

I wrote to you about hunting during the rut and I alluded to the hunter's infernal practice of rattling to confuse us and cause us to be at great risk. I thought I would write a separate letter about rattling since it is so important and dangerous to us.

You know that during the rut we bucks often find ourselves competing for the favors of the same doe. This often results in actual fights between two bucks. When this happens, it's a clear signal to every other buck within earshot (and that distance is great), that a fight is going on. An enterprising third buck could easily slip in and steal the affections of the doe from the two fighting bucks.

The sounds of two bucks fighting are rather characteristic. What with the scraping of bushes, hitting of horns, and the general commotion, there are no other sound combinations quite the same. When humans discovered this fact, they immediately recognized that if they could imitate the sounds they could fool us into thinking that their imitations were the real event. They were right. If done correctly, it will fool many of us. We cannot resist the temptation to investigate the action and get into the act.

The secret here is the quality of the imitation. A poor imitation of rattling will immediately tell every deer in the area that humans are fooling around trying to simulate a fight. The deer will depart.

A good imitation, however, will have success. What makes a good imitation? Well, first of all, experience of hearing a real fight will enable the hunter to reproduce the sound more accurately. Also, it really pays to learn the technique from an expert who has successfully rattled many times in the past. There are even tape recordings of rattling that a hunter can buy that will let him listen to the correct method.

Rattling techniques vary with the rattler. Each hunter does it a bit differently and will swear that his way is not only the best way but the only way. A hunter should learn from someone he trusts, observe closely, and also watch his success.

I told you about the Yankee who got into the taxicab in New York City and asked the driver if he knew how to get to Carnegie Hall. The driver answered, "Practice, practice, practice." Once the hunter has seen and heard how to rattle, he must practice until he has developed a successful technique. It will greatly help to choose a time when there is little wind and it is very quiet. This will allow the sound to travel farther. Finding a good place to hide while rattling that will still allow a good view is essential, especially down wind, because the deer may circle around down wind of the noise (if he has any common sense left). The hunter needs a good pair of horns to rattle that are also safe. He should cut off the sharp tips so that he doesn't injure himself when he smashes the horns together to simulate the sounds of fighting. He shouldn't hit the horns together over and over again for several minutes. Deer don't fight that way. Rather, brief rattling with frequent pauses will be successful. Also the hunter should rub on some nearby brush to sound authentic.

There is no way I can accurately describe how the sounds should be made. I must repeat, the hunter should not overdo the rattling noise and should wait a good long time between rattling episodes to allow the bucks to figure out there is a fight and to find it.

Now, Dad, let me remind you that bucks react to a good rattle with emotion, not intelligence. They will rush in without caution and run over anything in their way, including hidden hunters. I have seen some of my cousins almost impale hunters with their antlers, not on purpose, but because they were looking for the fight and didn't expect to find a human. Deer can come so close to the hunter that he can reach out and touch them, so close that he can't get a shot because he can't sight in that close. Deer will give him multiple opportunities for shots as they circle around the source of the rattling so if he doesn't panic, he may get the shot of his life and the buck of his dreams.

If hormones are dictating the buck's actions, then adrenaline is dictating the hunter's. When he rattles up a trophy buck, I guarantee the hunter will get so excited he won't be able to hold the rifle still. He had better make sure he has a good rest to help him steady his aim. He will be shaking so much that a free-hand shot will be impossible, and even a totally sandbagged rifle will probably shake, he will be so excited.

Hunters who have heard about rattling will want to utilize this valuable tool. The bad news is that rattling is worthless when there is no rut. Bucks not interested in does will have no desire to fight and will not "come to the horns".

It follows, therefore, that the hunter must know when the rut is taking place, and he must schedule at least part of his hunting during that period. Then, he should get ready for one of the truly exciting experiences of his life. I guess I've given away enough of our secrets for now. Take care of yourself and remember your age. When you hear bucks fighting over a doe, let them alone. You don't need to go see what's happening. Either way, you will lose. You may blunder into some hunters rattling and get shot. Worse, it may be a real fight and you might find the doe. Then what will you do? Dad, you're not getting any younger. I'm worried about your heart giving out although I suppose a heart attack is as good as any other way to go and certainly better than starving to death next winter.

Love,

Buck

Scrapes

Deer Dad:

I know that I wrote you a very long letter about rattling. I'm sorry it was so long, but that is a very important subject and it always gets me going. Today I thought I would write a little about scrapes. Don't worry, scrapes don't get me as excited. This letter will be shorter.

I said that scrapes don't get me excited, but, then, I'm not a hunter. I make scrapes naturally. Hunters, if they are smart, will look for scrapes as a guide to deer. There may be deer without scrapes, but there will not be scrapes without deer.

I know you know what a scrape is. I suspect you may have made thousands in your life. Were a hunter to read this letter, I would tell him that a scrape is a message. It is a method of communication between deer of the opposite sex. The message, quite simply, is, "I'm here; where are you?"

Making a scrape requires a definite system. First of all, the buck starts the process by finding a suitable location, suitable meaning there are some hanging tree limbs or bushes over the desired piece of ground. He then paws at the ground scraping into the dirt (hence the name). At the same time, he rubs the overlying branches with his antlers, usually removing the foliage from them. He also urinates into the scraped ground, making sure the urine washes over the tarsal glands on the inside of his hind legs, and then he goes his way.

A doe will then find the scrape, and smell the buck's urine. If she is receptive and interested in some "amour," she will urinate into the scrape and wait in the area. The buck returns, smells the doe's urine, and "whoopee."

Scrapes, therefore, really do serve as a method of communication between deer. The message does not have to be limited to deer. A clever hunter, able to recognize scrapes, to tell how fresh they are, and to leave them alone but still find a place to hide nearby, may be able to find a trophy buck and find him during a time when his attention may be diverted by more important instincts than survival.

107

More than one trophy has been obtained using what I call the "hormone approach."

By the way, deer urine has a significant odor, especially when mixed with the odor of secretions from the glands found on the hind legs. It is this combination of odors that attracts one deer to another. It is the same odor, or some imitation thereof, that some hunters use as scent to cover their human smell. I will write more about this later.

I told you this letter would be shorter. I know your attention span is not as long as it once was. By the way, I heard that fresh acorns will improve a problem with attention span. Try some. They can't hurt you, and they taste great.

Love,

Buck

I Smell Pretty

Deer Dad:

Humans smell. Believe it or not, Dad, if I were a human I would have insulted many people by making that statement. Fortunately, I am not and, even more fortunately, I have the proboscis (that means nose) and the olfactory apparatus that goes along with it to be considered fairly expert in the smelling department. You and I both know that, even though humans smell, so do all other animals. Not only do animals smell, but their odor is distinctive for the species.

Deer smell. A human who has some experience can easily detect the odor of deer when we are in the neighborhood. Although I have now established that humans and deer can smell each other, I am pleased to report that the deer's sense of smell is much more acute than human's. We can smell them from farther away and more easily than they can smell us.

That is an advantage that most humans find unacceptable and have, in fact, set out to take away from us. They have developed several tactics to even out the "smelly" difference.

First of all, they have learned about wind direction. Wind carries the smell of animals and humans along with it. It stands to reason that if the hunter, or the deer for that matter, can determine the direction of the wind and position himself downwind of whatever he wants to identify, then he should be able to detect the odor while his own scent will be undetectable (unless there is another adversary further downwind).

Another tactic developed by the humans is to remove their own human scent. There are materials they can wash with to try to achieve this, but it is really quite difficult to eliminate any scent since it's constantly being produced and gets into all their clothes. That doesn't mean they won't try.

It is easier to cover up human scent with the scent of some other animal. One of the smelliest animals is the skunk. Humans will go so far as to cover themselves with skunk scent to hide their own smell. It's my opinion that if this is what hunters wants to do, more power to them. I admire their fanaticism. I hope their wives like it.

Hunters can obtain deer scent and use it to cover up their own scent. This has the added advantage (they think) of not only hiding their own scent but also making us think they are deer. They can purchase chemicals that will make them smell like a buck, a doe, a doe in heat, and who knows what else. I've told you before, Dad, humans are strange creatures. I wonder what they would say if I actually acted like they were does in heat and tried to rut with them. That should make a great photograph.

Enough of this silliness. If hunters spend good money on materials like scents, then, as I mentioned to you before, I will strongly consider collecting these letters I am sending you and publishing them in a book. They would surely buy it. I'll write again soon.

Love,

Buck

Field Dressing

Deer Dad:

The weather here has been delightful. Rain and fog almost all day long makes for a carefree day. I hope your climate is the same.

I promised you a letter about field dressing. I think it's important for any humans who plan to hunt to know as much as possible about field dressing. It's essential to do it properly and, while it's not necessary to be a surgeon to do it correctly, a few points will help. Ending up with the best possible venison begins with proper field dressing.

First of all, let's get one thing straight. Who is responsible for field dressing? That's an easy question to answer-the hunter. A particularly generous host may offer to do this chore for the hunter but remember, it's the hunters problem.

Let me provide some hints from my observations of hunters and their misadventures. The hunter should first make sure the deer is dead before he starts the process. Sounds obvious, huh? Well believe me, there is nothing so surprising as walking up to a deer (especially a buck), grabbing hold of him to get him into a good position for field dressing only to have him wake up and scare the unsuspecting human so badly that he has to change his pants. It's also very dangerous. The only time to waste time in the field dressing process is before it starts so that the hunter doesn't encounter this problem.

I'm not about to give a step by step description of how to do this process. There are plenty of books available and the novice can always ask advice from an experienced hunter. I do have several tips.

A question the hunter must decide early on is whether or not he intends to make a mount of his deer. If he does, he cannot make as long an incision into the chest and neck. If he is not sure what he wants to do about mounting, it's best to field dress as if he were going to visit the taxidermist.

He should make sure he has a good, sharp knife with a long blade. This is not a job for a pocket knife or one recently used to chop down trees.

The hunter should make sure the deer is in a good stable position on his back or hanging from a suitable high support so that he will not flop around during the process. Usually the deer will be on the ground so he should be stabilized at the top with his head and his antlers. The hunter should then stand on the deer's rear legs to prevent movement during the field dressing process.

The hunter should get comfortable. He will probably be bent over for a while. He will get warm, so he should take off some of his heavy clothing before he starts. Things will probably get messy, and he will not want to soil his clothing during the process by touching them with his hands.

He must make a careful incision in the midline through the abdominal skin and fatty tissue beneath it, taking care not to cut so deeply that he enters the intestines. The incision should extend to completely encircle the rectum. If he has tools that will divide the symphysis pubis (the heavy bone near the deer's genitalia) such as a saw, it is a good idea to do it to prevent the possibility of entering the large bowel.

When he reaches into the chest to divide the large blood vessels above the heart, the fun really starts. He will find blood. He should feel around first before he cuts anything so that when he does cut he will be ready to do it decisively and pull the heart and lungs away quickly. He will have to cut the diaphragm muscle separating the abdomen and chest on each side and then remove the rest of the contents by pulling them toward the hind legs of the animal.

After he has removed the internal organs, the hunter should turn the deer over to drain out as much blood as possible. He should avoid getting the blood all over himself and all over the deer since it will be difficult to remove later.

By the way, in most places the hunter is required to tag the deer in the field as soon as possible after shooting him. In order to tag the deer, he has to acquire a license with the attached tags BEFORE he starts hunting. To wait until he shoots a deer invites more than just a lecture from his local game warden.

If he is smart, the hunter will find a way to clean up as quickly as possible not only himself but his knife as well. Some hunters and landowners have inexpensive field dressing kits that contain many nice features to make the process easier. These kits will often include a pair of plastic gloves as well as a towelette to clean up afterwards and even a little antiseptic cream in case the hunter cuts himself.

Experienced hunters can field dress a deer in just a few minutes, some in even less then a minute from the incision to the draining of the body cavity. It's best not to get too close to these "minute men." The observer may end up part of the dressed animal. It's not really necessary to do it that fast unless the human is trying to impress someone. With experience, anyone can improve his time and accuracy.

With any luck we will not be on the end of somebody's knife, but if we are, I hope it's done well. Take care of yourself, stay hidden, and eat a well balanced diet. I want you around to read my letters.

Love,

Buck

How Old Am I?

Deer Dad:

I hope you are well. Good health is so important. I realize this more as I get older. You know how hard it is to get doctors to make "field" calls anymore.

You may remember in previous letters I have discussed appropriate game management. The aim is to obtain the best possible trophy herd and then harvest it properly. "Appropriately" means to shoot the oldest animals. They are usually the ones with the best racks anyway so they should be the ideal trophy. The older animals will find it hardest to survive the winter. Shooting young males and then having the old males die of natural causes after the season makes no sense. All the landowner ends up with is a decimated buck population.

Talking about shooting old deer and doing it are two different things. First of all, how does the hunter tell how old a deer is when he is looking at him and deciding on a shot? Size may help some, but once a deer reaches maturity he remains about the same size for several years. A good hunter will not shoot a small buck that is not a spike.

Antler configuration helps determine age some since as a deer matures his rack will usually increase in size and configuration. A buck with small antlers that is not a spike should not be shot.

The only accurate way to determine the age of a deer is to examine his tooth structure. As a deer gets older, his teeth wear down from all the chewing. Wildlife managers who have studied many animals have classified tooth configuration by age so that careful examination of the teeth will accurately tell the age of the animal. Unfortunately, it is very difficult to do this type of examination before the animal is shot. Walking up to a deer and telling him to "say ah" just won't work. On the other hand, a serious hunter will examine the teeth of every dead deer he can to practice aging the animal. Various books with photographs and drawings of deer teeth configurations can be used as references. There are also models available which can allow practice in aging.

While this doesn't help tell the age of the live deer, comparison of all these factors will help give a feel or sixth sense about the age of the live deer while evaluating him in the field.

Well, Dad, we know about your age. Thanks to the quality of hunters on your property, you have survived many years. I wish there were deer dentists available to help both of us with a new set of dentures. There's no telling how long we could survive if we had a new set of teeth. Unfortunately, it's our teeth that will do us in and starvation doesn't sound very healthy. I guess we better enjoy it while we can.

Take care of yourself. I will write again soon.

Love,

Buck

I Taste Good

Deer Dad:

I know I just wrote to you about old age. I am writing more frequently then before and I suppose it's a result of my concern about the future.

I want to write a little about tradition. Tradition is what makes the world stable. We do things that our parents did as they did things that their parents did before them. Humans have even written plays about tradition. One is called *Fiddler on the Roof* and it had a classic song about tradition. It's best not to ask where traditions started because there are usually no answers to that question. They exist, and that's enough.

You know, the biggest tradition among landowners, passed on from father to son, is to not kill does. We have already discussed that tradition, but there are many others. Some actually fall into the category of superstitions.

It is hunting tradition that the men hunt the deer and the women cook the venison. Actually, some of the best hunters I have seen are women, and some of the best venison I have eaten has been cooked by men. Now, Dad, you know that's a little joke. I am not a cannibal, but I have listened carefully to the men talking in the camphouse after a day's hunting. They will often describe the delicious recipes they have prepared and always claim that they can cook better than their wives. I've never seen them do it, however.

When a hunter's wife does cook venison, and if that dish is not up to par or to the expectations of the hunter, then the poor lady never hears the end of it. If the hunter realized that poorly prepared venison is probably due to mishandling the meat before he ever got it home, he would be embarrassed. He should be, because it's usually his fault.

There are many traditions that should be followed if the hunter is trying to end up with the best possible meat from his deer. First of all, there is the proper way to field dress a deer. I have already written to you about this. The hunter must remember that field dressing means just that. It must be done in the field and it must be done as quickly as possible after the deer is killed. No excuses! No squeamishness! He has to do it correctly and do it right away. I know it may be getting dark by then, or it may be getting hot. At best, it is uncomfortable and messy. That's part of the deal. An important tradition is the hunter who shoots the deer field dresses it. It gets the job done quickly and will go a long way toward producing the best meat.

When he gets the dressed deer back to camp, the hunter needs to make sure he has done a good job in the field and then wash the inside and outside of the carcass completely. He must get rid of all the blood from inside the chest and abdominal cavity and from the outside hide as well. Then, the deer must be hung from some suitable device so that the water can drain completely.

Now the hunter has a basic decision to make. He can skin the animal himself and even butcher, wrap, and freeze the meat, or he can get an expert to do it for him. The deer should be aged for a time and then processed correctly. I don't think the hunter should be a hero. He should let the experts do it and pay them their fee for this processing. He will be happier in the long run. He can also have the butcher prepare sausage or chili meat or any other delicacies in his repertoire.

Whatever else happens, the hunter doesn't need to sling the deer across the front of his car for the drive home. It's not impressive and will almost guarantee ruining the meat and probably his car as well.

Deciding about the cuts of meat is important. Almost everyone likes the backstraps or what would correspond to the fillet of beef. The human may prefer to make all the rest of the meat into chili or he may want the usual cuts that would correspond to beef cuts. He should remember to have the meat properly prepared for storage which usually means wrapped for the freezer. He should also remember to use the meat in a timely fashion and avoid freezer burn.

If the deer is properly field dressed, the hunter will avoid most of the causes of ruined meat. By the way, there are glands on the hind legs near the lower leg joint. They are brown areas on the hide. Some people feel that these glands should be removed as quickly as possible not to ruin the meat. I'm not sure it makes any difference, but if I were a hunter I certainly would not hesitate to take this step in case these "experts" are correct.

One last thing. The preparation of the meat is important. Poor preparation is what the hunter's wife gets blamed for if the venison is not up to par. There are many recipes available. Some use marinades, some do not. Every hunter is sure that if very specific traditions are not followed in the kitchen, the meat will be ruined. There are so many varied recipes that I am sure it doesn't make any difference. The hunter should leave his wife alone and let her cook it the way she wants.

That's my unsolicited advice about preparing venison. Again, I realize I'm probably cutting my own throat, but if I'm going to be eaten some day, I want to taste as good as I can. I know this is a depressing subject so after you read this letter go out and eat some tender oats and don't worry.

Love,

Buck

Mounting Your Trophy

Deer Dad:

I still can't believe what I saw yesterday. It was so unusual that I thought I would write to you immediately and tell you about it. By the way, I hope you are doing well.

I am constantly amazed at the strange behavior of some humans. I was wandering about yesterday, daydreaming a bit. You know that daydreaming is very dangerous business in the middle of hunting season. I will admit I got a little too far from home. I tell you I won't do that again. I found myself near the fence line of the adjoining property. All of a sudden, I heard a shot. After making sure that it wasn't aimed at me, I decided to investigate a little further. I saw a hunter examining a handsome buck, one of our distant cousins, in the next pasture. The deer had a fine rack, some twelve points with a good spread and high tines. A few minutes later, one of the hunter's friends appeared in a pickup truck. They discussed the deer and I heard the first hunter offer the head, obviously a trophy, to the second hunter, saying he was only interested in the meat. Naturally, the second hunter gladly obliged. I'm sure he intended to claim the trophy as his own.

Dad, what I don't understand is why the first hunter didn't want the trophy and why he didn't get it mounted. It's indeed strange that once having killed such a beautiful animal he did not want to display it on his wall.

Anyway, that hunter is in the distinct minority. Most hunters would gladly bear the expense of mounting. Since this is the case, I thought it best to go over a few points about mounting game in case any human finds this letter eventually.

The first decision the hunter has to make is whether to have the animal mounted professionally or to try to do it himself. Notice I used the word try. It is actually quite difficult and truly an art to do taxidermy, which is what humans call mounting game. I will admit that there are kits available for the amateur taxidermist and, of course, there are many books published on the subject, but believe me, Dad, there is much more to it than just reading a book and starting out. I would strongly advise any hunter to let the experts deal with the mounting process.

Be that as it may, there are several steps a hunter must take to be sure that, regardless of who mounts the game, the animal is properly delivered to maximize the quality of the job. First of all, the hunter has to shoot the deer correctly. The best place to shoot a deer, especially a trophy, is in the heart. The heart is located just behind the front shoulder about two-thirds from the top of the back or one-third from the bottom. It is the one place that is surest to kill the animal with the least amount of suffering and at the same time keep large holes out of the area to be included in the mount. Humans have spent many hours debating the best place to shoot a deer. Some advocate shooting the deer in the spine, some, the head, and some, the neck. The heart is the best place. Other anatomical areas will result in a higher incidence of merely wounding. Besides, while taxidermists can work miracles fixing up unsightly holes and other damage, it's better to provide them an unmarred animal.

Correct field dressing is important when considering mounting. It is much easier to field dress a deer by making an incision from the very bottom of the abdomen to the top of the chest and into the neck, but such a high incision will destroy some of the cape that the taxidermist will need to make a good looking mount. If mounting the deer is a possibility, it is best to make an incision only to the beginning of the chest cavity and reach up to divide the major blood vessels above the heart by feel rather than sight.

The deer should then be skinned properly by removing the skin and subcutaneous tissue but leaving behind the fat. Enough skin should be removed to allow the taxidermist to mount the head and upper body. This should include the skin over the rib cage at least. The head should be separated where it is attached to the spine and left attached to the skin. The head and cape should be taken to the taxidermist as rapidly as possible but it should be frozen unless this can be done immediately.

The hunter should be prepared to discuss the details of the type of mount desired with the taxidermist. The deer can be mounted facing directly forward or with the head turned either right or left with varying degrees of twist. The hunter should plan the mounting based upon where in the room the trophy will be hung as well as its relationship to other items already on display.

Then the hunter should sit back and wait. Hunting season lasts only a few short weeks (thank the Lord), and many hunters will want their trophies mounted. All of them cannot be first in line. It certainly pays to have patience rather than trying to rush and ending up with an inferior job.

All this talk of mounting gets me depressed. I better end this letter now before I decide not to send it.

Love,

Buck

Send This Boy to Camp

Deer Dad:

It occurs to me that you may not have been able to get around too much lately. I know that your arthritis is acting up, and I suppose that for the last few years your travels have been quite limited. I wish there were some hot springs on your property. The warm mineral water certainly would do wonders for you. You could bathe at night and feel refreshed all day. Perhaps those human doctors will soon find a cure for arthritis. It would help both men and deer. I will talk to some of our cousins from Minnesota. The Mayo Clinic should certainly be able to help.

Anyway, I really wanted to tell you about some of the different types of camps these hunters live in when they come out to "rough it" during the hunting season. Camps come in all types and varieties, ranging from the simple to the luxurious.

Humans are really quite inconsistent about their living requirements. When they are at "home," they demand the best type of living accommodations they can possibly afford. Often, they choose accommodations they cannot afford. I've never seen any of their city homes, but (from magazines I have read) they are really something. They have many rooms of varied types. Some of them are where they sleep. They sleep on funny things called beds. Actually they are big bags filled with soft stuff like we use—pine needles, leaves, and other soft things, I guess. Some of the bags are filled with water. Very strange. They have rooms where they eat, others where they watch something called television, which I don't understand at all, and even rooms called bathrooms—I won't even try to tell you what they do there.

When they go hunting, these same humans often prefer to live just opposite from the way they do at home. They choose tents, huts, small metal buildings on wheels they call trailers, and, sometimes, nothing. They just sleep outside, like we do. I think they feel if they inconvenience themselves and live entirely differently than they normally would that will improve their hunting.

I think they call it "communing with nature." Most often all they commune with is mosquitoes. Occasionally, they commune with dangerous animals such as snakes, bears, and other beasts who do not fear the human and whose curiosity draws these species into confrontation with the humans.

Now there are some humans who don't have this curious need to "rough it" and actually understand that hunting should be approached scientifically rather than emotionally. If they can afford it, they usually set up a camp that is as comfortable as possible and as their finances will allow. They realize that the time not spent in the field should be spent in preparing to go into the field. Hearty meals for nourishment's sake and a good night's sleep for alertness' sake are essential ingredients to a successful hunt. They will often duplicate their city type dwellings and have running water, indoor toilets, and that ubiquitous television for relaxation. I will write you more about the food they eat and how they relax in other letters.

Love,

Buck

Camphouse Talk

Deer Dad:

How are you? I hope this warm weather isn't bothering you too much. Winter will be here before you know it so take advantage of the heat while you can.

You know, in my travels I have had a good chance to listen to humans and read their books. I have learned some very interesting things. It's very easy to listen to them. They talk all the time. They talk in their houses. They talk in their vehicles. They even talk while they hunt. I guess that's just their way of playing fair and letting us know where they are. They talk at night, also, when they get together after their day's activities so they can brag about their achievements. I think they call that "lying." Humans spend time in their camphouses talking along with drinking some liquid most often referred to as beer, eating, and doing just about everything but planning for their next day's hunting activities.

From my point of view, there is nothing more enjoyable than sneaking up to these camphouses and listening to the humans talking with each other. I will tell you some of the things I have learned by listening to them. First of all, I know what stocks to buy. Actually, I know what stocks not to buy. I think humans take great pleasure in convincing other humans to join them in investments—something about "misery liking company." The peculiar thing is I never hear about bad stocks, only good ones. I guess there is no such thing as a bad stock.

I can also tell you that the world in general is a terrible place for humans. Things are always bad. There is always a war going on. The places usually change from season to season, but I learned that humans like to hunt each other as much as they like to hunt us.

Also, there are always big problems in some place called Washington. Apparently, some of the human's leaders are not as good as others. They don't always play fair with each other. Actually, to a human, playing fair means doing things just the way he wants them done. Anything else is unfair to him. We better not go anywhere near Washington. These Washington humans are not nice people, and we can't trust them with anything but tax money. Of course, deer don't pay taxes, so we shouldn't have anything to worry about, but I did hear one human announce that he heard the government is trying to figure out a way to tax us also.

I will tell you more about what I have heard soon. I do want to tell you now what I have not heard in the camphouses. I have not heard humans tell each other where the good places to hunt are located, where they know deer are guaranteed to be present. Even though some of them have clearly determined where we hide during the day, they never seem to tell each other this valuable information. They must honestly forget to tell each other because when they find our hiding places they sure are happy.

Oh, well, humans are sometimes hard to figure out. Take care of yourself. I'll write again soon.

Love,

Buck

Camphouse Etiquette

Deer Dad:

I hope you are well. I guess it must seem strange to you that I am so worried about you now after not having even spoken to you for all those years. I guess I have matured some since those wild days of my youth.

You know, I never get over the strange antics of these humans. They have laws to govern themselves. If they break the laws, then they put each other into small dens with bars on the front so they can't get out. Even so, they try and try to get out and sometimes succeed.

They also have "rules" that are not as strong as laws but seem important to follow anyway. They sometimes call these rules "etiquette." It's especially important to follow them when hunting. Apparently, there have been times when hunters have been less civilized with each other and these rules were developed to prevent loss of friendship between the hunters.

Therefore, how hunters behave in their hunting camps is very significant and has achieved a ritual status. A new hunter should be very careful not to break any of the rules. Sometimes these rules are actually written down. Most of the time they are unwritten but crucial just the same.

One of the most important rules seems to deal with camp food cooking and eating. The quality of food served in hunting camps varies greatly. It largely depends upon the circumstances of the camp arrangements. In the really posh camps, usually those that invite guests, a cook will prepare the food for all the hunters. In other camps, usually those under lease, the hunters may themselves cook. They may appoint one hunter as permanent cook, or rotate the privilege. Sometimes they may bring along a known non-hunter and award him the "honor" of cooking.

The rule is NEVER CRITICIZE THE FOOD. I heard an interesting story about this once. In one camp, where the cooking chores were rotated among all the hunters, the rule was that if anyone criticized the food, he had to take over the cooking. Naturally, no one wanted this duty, even the present cook. He decided to try to do his worst so that someone would complain and he could get out of the cooking job. As badly as he prepared the food, no one complained because no one wanted the job. One day the cook took some fresh cow manure and made it into hamburger patties. One hunter took a bite and involuntarily exclaimed, "This tastes like manure." Realizing what he said, he quickly added "But good manure."

Generally, there is considerable discussion on a wide variety of topics in a hunting camp. There are some topics that are dangerous to discuss and hunters, even if they are close friends, should be very careful when discussing them. It is considered bad form to talk about subjects that might prove embarrassing to other hunters. That is not to say that humorous stories, often at the expense of one or more of the hunters in camp, are not often and elaborately told, but there are still some subjects that should be discussed delicately, if at all.

One of these subjects is politics. Nothing is calculated to cause more instant hate among humans than discussions regarding politics. Apparently, a man's politics is as important as his religion. In fact, Dad, religion is the other topic that should be avoided in camp, at least for the neophyte hunter or newly invited guest.

I have tried and tried to understand what this politics and religion stuff is all about. All I can tell is it must be very important to the humans because when they do discuss these subjects they often shout and yell and go away angry. Oh well, I'll keep listening and maybe some day I'll figure it out.

There are some good subjects to discuss in camp. Sharing hunting tips and past experiences seems to be very popular. Humans yell and shout when they discuss these things also. In fact humans often yell and shout when they discuss anything, but at camp all the commotion seems to be taken in good humor. Apparently, everyone has a vast past experience, and they are all extremely knowledgeable about hunting techniques, and they all love to share them with each other. As soon as one person tells a story, another has a better one. I have listened to these conversations as well. As a matter of fact, some of the stories are reasonably good and a few even seem accurate.

Humans also tell these things called jokes. They are usually short stories that don't have much meaning to me but when a human tells one of the stories the others usually laugh and then another human tells another one and this can go on for a long time. I intend to keep listening to these jokes and when they start to make sense to me, I'll save them up and send you some.

This etiquette business can get very complicated and tedious. There are a huge number of rules to remember. No human really has the mental capacity to remember them all and I can tell that emotion and ill feeling is created from time to time when a human forgets one of the rules. All in all, I think it's probably better to be a deer. The rules are simple and, as long as we are careful, we can stay out of trouble.

Love,

Buck

O.K. So What Else is There to Do?

Deer Dad:

You're not going to believe this but I was nosing around the outside of my human's camphouse the other day when I heard one of them say that he really didn't want to hunt and he wondered what else there was to do to keep busy. This was quite startling to me for two reasons.

First of all, I couldn't imagine why anyone would not want to hunt deer. I mean, even if he didn't want to shoot us, a position which I could easily imagine, he could at least hunt us with a camera as I have discussed with you before. This guy didn't want to sit in a blind and even look at us as we passed. This seems very strange, but you already know that these humans are strange.

The other thing I couldn't imagine is that he didn't think there was anything else to do around my ranch to keep busy. Actually, we both know that there are many things to do around a ranch both day and night, not only to keep busy but to actually have fun and become educated at the same time.

I thought I would write about some of the more common activities just to remind you of them because I know you do not get around as much as you once did and you may not have spied on your hunters recently.

First, we have sunrises and sunsets. If the weather is at all clear, these are truly beautiful sights on most any ranch and although sunrise is early in the morning, it's worth getting up to see. Sunset is much more popular with most humans because they already are up, but both sunrise and sunset are worthy of watching by the hunter and non-hunter alike.

Most ranches have abundant flora to study. There are generally trees, bushes, cacti, plants, and vegetation that can be most interesting and educational. Likewise, there are a multitude of animals around ranches that may or may not be candidates for hunting but are all worthy of observation. Some of the plants and animals on ranches are there because the owner is growing them

133

for market or some other use and this aspect of ranch activity is often interesting.

The more active humans may enjoy fishing since most ranches have water tanks or streams stocked with fish. Swimming is also a possibility, as is horseback riding, hiking, jogging, and many other physical fitness activities. There is always bird watching and hunting, animal calling, using any of a variety of man-made devices designed to fool animals into coming to see what's going on, and a host of other activities that will keep even the most citified human interested.

In the evenings there are many things to do. There are stars in the heavens that seem to take on a totally different appearance away from the bright lights of the human's cities, They are brighter and more easily seen. In some cities, I am told, stars cannot be seen at all.

Then, of course, the humans, being as inventive as they are, have their own man-made activities after it's too dark to hunt. When they should be preparing for the next day's hunt, they are instead doing things like playing card games, other types of games, swapping lies, watching television, drinking strange smelling drinks, and generally trying to have fun. Eventually they sleep, but usually wake up very tired.

Enough for now. I will write again soon.

Love,

Buck

Financial Arrangements

Deer Dad:

I was listening to my hunters talking the other night. As you know, a large part of their conversations deal with money. Money is something humans need and never have enough. Apparently, it takes money to do just about everything they like to do. I'm still not completely sure what money is. As I mentioned in an earlier letter, I think it's little pieces of green paper with pictures and writing on both sides. Sometimes, money is little round metal things that makes noise when you shake it around in a jar or some other type of container.

I mentioned a jar because in my experience money seems to come in jars. At least there is always a jar full of money on the table in the camphouse on my ranch. I suppose money is saved in other places as well, but a jar is the only place I've seen large accumulations.

The jar in the camphouse on my ranch is labeled "missed shots." Every time a new hunter comes to the ranch, the "old timers" explain the rules about the jar to him. Apparently, a hunter must put in a dollar each time he fires a shot and no meat is brought home. That means that if a hunter fires three shots at some type of game and does not eventually kill and find the animal, he has to place three dollars into the jar.

Now, Dad, when you think about it, that's a pretty good deal for the landowner. There is money in the jar, and, it seems to me, the more money in the jar, the better off we are, also. There are even pieces of money in the jar with the numbers twenty and fifty on them.

On my ranch, the landowner uses the money to buy things for the camp and for future hunting use. One year he bought a very well-built knife sharpener. This year there seems to be enough money in the jar to buy even very expensive items. As long as he doesn't buy books on how to hunt, I guess I will be happy, unless these letters are ever made into a book. Then I do hope he will spend some of the money in the jar to buy several copies for all the hunters on the ranch.

Some hunters will go to extremes to avoid putting money into the jar. One year, one of the hunters wounded a deer late in the evening, and although he tried mightily to find him, night fell and the deer was not recovered. (Dad, I'll write a separate letter about finding wounded deer.)

Now, the average human would have put his dollar into the jar and given up. Not this hunter. The next morning he continued the search, even on horseback. He remained unsuccessful. The rest of the hunters felt sorry for him. They tried to convince him that he missed the shot completely and the deer ran off and therefore would never be found. Some of them even offered to put a dollar into the jar for him, but he remained steadfast in his search. Finally, as a last resort, he brought in a helicopter to look for the deer he knew he wounded. After a brief trip in the helicopter he did locate the deer and brought him back to camp. Naturally, he did not have to put any money into the jar. He was very happy about that, not only because he found the deer, and he was a very nice deer, but also because he saved a dollar. I'm not sure how much he spent on the helicopter, but apparently that didn't matter.

I have learned from happenings such as this that humans have rather strange attitudes about money and other financial matters. They really do spend a huge amount of money to finance this sport. It would be interesting to try to place a dollar figure on the venison, per pound, that is harvested each year. If they think such food as beef and caviar are expensive, they would really be amazed at the cost of venison.

Oh well, that's part of the confusing activity in which humans participate. It really has very little touch with reality. It is much easier being a deer, and with the exception of hunting season, it's a lot more fun.

Now, Dad, I want you to take care of yourself. If your arthritis starts acting up, why don't you try a few of those mushrooms that grow over in that west pasture on your ranch? I think they would help you, but don't eat too many or they may make you sick.

Love,

Buck

Which Way Did He Go?

Deer Dad:

I must warn you that this is a morbid letter. Don't read any farther if you are depressed. Humans commit crimes. Many of the crimes are very serious. They even kill each other over the strangest circumstances. First of all, they have organized killing; they call that war. Then, they have spontaneous killing over such things as hate, love, greed, and a whole host of other crazy motives. Of course, there are a great many other crimes that are not quite as serious. They steal from each other, assault each other, gamble, forge checks, rape, and generally violate each other's civil liberties.

Of all their crimes, the one that ranks up there with the worst is wounding a deer and not finding him. Wounding a deer, even mortally, will usually cause the animal to run away from the spot in an attempt to flee the hunter. Rarely, unless the wound involves the nervous system, will he drop at the spot where he was shot.

In fact, animals only slightly wounded may completely disappear from the scene only to die later and farther away than initially imaginable. Still, it is clearly the hunter's responsibility to find the wounded animal and finish the job. It is the humane thing to do. The trouble is, humans are not always humane.

First of all, they may get tired and not have the stamina to find the animal. Also, they may not have the knowledge of how to do it properly. Worst of all, they may just not care enough about finding the animal and finishing the job. That's the reprehensible part.

Since I prefer to think kindly of humans, even though I know I'm often wrong, I would like to share with you some of the facts they should learn in order to track a wounded deer successfully and not get lost themselves. Then, Dad, I would appreciate it if you would lose this letter where a human can find it or at least save it in case I do write the book I keep threatening.

The usual scenario is that the hunter shoots a deer, wounds him, and the animal runs away. The first mistake commonly made is that the hunter immediately starts to run from the spot he was

137

shooting toward where he thinks the deer is lying, confident that he couldn't miss a shot and that he will find the deer right there. When he does this he scares the wounded animal into running farther and faster than he normally would and simply makes it harder to find the deer.

A cardinal rule, espoused by all experts yet consistently ignored, is that the hunter should wait at least fifteen minutes after shooting a deer before beginning to look for it. Sounds crazy, right? It is good advice. The idea is to let the deer run a bit, then stop to rest and evaluate his situation. He will think he is safe if he doesn't perceive activity and may stay down allowing the shot to take its effect. Some human experts also believe that allowing the animal to rest rather than exert excess energy and adrenaline running away will make the meat tastier later on.

So, the hunter should wait a full fifteen minutes and then cautiously walk, slowly and deliberately, toward the spot he last saw the deer. While he is waiting, the hunter should have ample opportunity to recall the details of the shot he just made and mark clearly in his head the spot where the deer was standing. While walking slowly to the spot, he should constantly scan the area looking not only for the deer, but also for any signs the deer left, particularly blood. Finding and following blood is an excellent way to track a wounded deer, but the hunter must remember that there may only be a few drops here and there and they may be spread far apart. He shouldn't just rummage around the area but walk slowly in a particular pattern carefully lest he disturb the evidence. He may also be able to find tracks the fleeing deer left behind. He should remember the wounded deer will be running and digging into the ground deeply in order to get away as quickly as possible. Although there may be many tracks in the area, a deer running for his life will have deep tracks farther apart than normal.

Just because the hunter wants him to, the deer may not run in a straight line but may change direction frequently in his attempt to get away. The hunter, now tracker, should follow the tracks and blood spots carefully, looking for blood not only on the ground but also on foliage and grass. Blood may be found in increasing or decreasing amounts depending upon the part of the animal wounded and the nature of the wound.

The hunter should gradually follow the trail, remembering that the deer may have stopped just ahead and, if spooked, will only get up and run again until all his strength in gone. Spooking should be avoided at all costs, since it only makes tracking longer and makes it harder to find the animal. If he moves slowly and carefully, just as he would if he were "still hunting," the hunter will minimize this risk.

When he spots the deer—the hunter should freeze and evaluate the situation. Is the deer dead? He may look dead, but if still alive may either run away when the hunter approaches or even injure the hunter when he walks up to the deer and reaches for his rack. Is he alive? It would then be appropriate to carefully shoot him again to end his misery. If the hunter is not sure, he should assume the deer is still alive. Another shot won't hurt and won't even count against him if his camp has a penalty rule of money in the jar for missed shots. He will bring home the deer.

The tracking process may take several hours if the deer has moved any great distance. That's all right. The hunter must give tracking time it needs.

What should he do if he can't find any trace of the animal? The idea is to assume he hit the deer and keep looking. One way is for the hunter to move slowly in the direction he thinks the deer went, or if he is completely lost, move in increasing concentric circles. If help arrives, it is essential to organize the patterns appropriately so that he and his friends are not working at cross purposes. Searching from horseback may help and from a helicopter is also a very good way to find the deer. Dogs also are able to find dead dear from the scent, but all these methods require significant support that is usually not available. If unsuccessful, the hunter may find some remains a few days later when the buzzards can be seen circling and feeding.

Above all, it's a good idea for the hunter not to get lost himself during this process. Depending upon the geography of the property, getting lost may be easier than it sounds. I will write how to avoid this in future letters.

That's about enough for now. I hope the letter didn't bother you too much. It is an important subject. I will write again soon.

Love,

Buck

Better Safe Than Sorry

Deer Dad:

I have just about decided that human hunters are crazy. I know that's a harsh term, but I think it must be true. I can't tell you about how many countless bullet holes I have seen in doors, windows, roofs, and even oil pans of trucks. That's right Dad, oil pans. Oil pans are on the underneath of trucks. A hunter has to shoot through the floor, miss several other things, and then hit the oil pan on the bottom. It's not easy, but these humans are very clever.

Shooting a truck is not good. Not only does it damage the truck, often requiring significant money to repair, but after a hunter shoots a truck it is very hard to field dress. Then, of course, if he shoots a truck, he has considerable explaining to do when all his friends find out.

I have also seen cows, barns, houses, windmills, and just about every other type of object shot. Believe it or not, Dad, I have even seen a human shot. Somehow, humans look like deer to other humans. I don't know why. To me, a deer is a deer and a human is a human.

You would think these humans would understand the basic safety concept that they must see what they are shooting. It's not a good idea to shoot at moving branches, sounds, or other un-identified objects. I know how excited they get, but shooting without knowing what they are shooting at is a real shame. Actually, in human terms it is indeed a crime.

Humans' ideas of safety in general are crazy. They put themselves in dangerous positions and don't even take the basic precautions that are immediately available.

Did you ever hear of a seat belt? Humans install them in vehicles so if they have an accident they won't get thrown out and get seriously injured. They install seat belts but rarely use them. Humans love to stand in the back of trucks to hunt better and then love to go "hell bent for leather" all over the countryside at unsafe speeds just hoping they will get thrown out. I haven't even brought up the subject of motorcycles.

All of this aside, the average human's knowledge of gun safety is nil. You should see them walking, climbing, running, and doing all kinds of other activities with live shells in the chambers of their rifles, safeties off, pointing the rifles everywhere but where they should be pointed. It's a wonder that more humans don't get shot.

It's not so bad when hunters on any given property are limited in number so that they can keep far away from each other, but on some properties, especially public lands, they literally crawl all over each other in search of their prey.

All of this is to warn you to be careful. It's one thing to be shot after some smart hunter works hard to get you. It's entirely another to be shot accidentally and even worse to be run over by a car or something. Stay hidden and let the humans hunt each other. It's better for everyone.

Love,

Buck

If It Moves, Shoot It?

Deer Dad:

I'm glad to hear you are doing well. I know you haven't written, but I did hear from an antelope passing by that he saw you. Speaking of seeing, I want to write you a letter about seeing and, specifically, seeing before shooting.

You know very well that if we, the hunted, can't be seen, then it's not likely that we will be shot, that is, of course, in the normal situation when we are wise enough to live on land populated by prudent hunters. That is the key to survival—picking the best place to live. We can't get away from hunters. They are everywhere. The best we can hope for is to live where hunters understand game management and know hunting is a sport, not a war.

So, from our point of view, we have to stay out of sight of the hunter. Most of us do this quite well. It's when we fail, for whatever reason, that we pay the price.

So much for you and me. There are many of our relatives who are neither as smart or as lucky. They live where the crazy hunters are. There are some hunters who will shoot at anything, even if they can't see what they are shooting and even if they are not sure there is anything to shoot.

I have watched some of them and heard stories as well. Many things in the field confuse the hunter and unless he has some experience or self control, he ends up being a danger to us, other hunters, and even to himself.

Moving bushes is a classic example of a hunter's misguided target. When the wind blows nearby bushes, some hunters think that there is an animal of some sort moving the bushes instead of the wind. What harm can there be in taking s shot at a moving bush? None, I suppose, if it really is the wind, some, if there really is an animal and the hunter scares him away, and a great deal, if it's some other human in the bushes causing them to move. In some places, especially where there is public hunting and the hunter can go anywhere on the property, it is very common for another hunter

143

to be in the bushes intent on finding some game. Each year, many humans are killed by careless hunters shooting at moving bushes. When this happens, all sorts of problems occur for the humans involved. Not is only killing another human considered bad, but field dressing him is even worse. Field dressing does not happen often, but, there is a group of humans, all graduates from some type of agricultural school in Texas, that seems to be blamed for this type of activity. It's as if they didn't know any better.

If moving bushes are a problem for hunters so are trees and cacti. Especially in the early dawn or late dusk, hunters think the natural foliage looks more and more like game. Windmills are also confusing to humans, strange as that may seem; they often get littered with bullet holes. Game feeders also receive the same treatment. Even road signs along the highways get bullet holes, especially the signs that warn humans of deer crossings. It seems the humans like to shoot at them, for practice I think.

Cows are also a problem for hunters. It may be hard for you to understand, Dad. I don't think a cow looks like a deer to you or me, but to a hunter, especially a novice or one that gets excited easily, cows can be confusing. I heard of one landowner who painted the letters "COW" on the sides of all his cattle because he was worried that some hunter might make a mistake. I hope he used an oil base paint; it's a long season.

I have strayed from the subject. I find myself doing that more and more as I get older. I have to watch that. Finally, there are some other animals that are not generally considered game that are confusing for the hunters. Dogs and other small domesticated animals are often found on ranches, and hunters should avoid shooting them. They often belong to the owner of the property, and he might take offense if someone were to kill his pet.

The bottom line, as humans like to say, is for hunters to remember that they should never shoot anything unless they can clearly identify what they are shooting, and then only when they have a clear shot. Otherwise, it's much wiser not to shoot at game at all but just shoot at each other.

I will write again soon.

Love,

Buck

Get Lost

Deer Dad:

Humans have developed a machine to record whatever they can see and show it on a screen or other flat surface. It's called a movie. I once saw a movie showing where many humans live. They call them cities. Cities are usually very big places with many buildings. It would be very easy for me to get lost in one of those cities. Thankfully, I don't have to worry about that because I will never be in one of them. I intend to stay very close to home, and I know my way around here very well.

It's interesting, Dad, that while I will never get lost in the humans' city, humans will often get lost in our territory. I suppose if they did the same as we and just stayed in their natural habitat, neither of us would have a problem. That's not the way it is in this world. They will come to our territory each and every fall, just as regular as clockwork.

They will come, and some of them will get lost. In fact, so many of them get lost that I wonder why they don't take a few simple precautions and learn about the territory before they venture into the unknown.

Maps are great. They can really orient the hunter to the property. They should be studied before going out and getting disoriented. Most every piece of land is mapped and has all the appropriate landmarks. Most property owners would be happy to provide hunters with these maps because they don't want the hunter lost anymore than the hunter wants to get lost.

It's best for a hunter's first experience with a property not to go out before dawn on the first day of his hunting trip. A tour of the property during daylight hours, preferably with someone knowledgeable about the property, would be most appropriate.

Then, of course, there are helpful hints the hunter should remember if he does get lost or thinks he is lost. He should remember that for a long time now the sun has risen in the east and set in the west. Following the path of the sun, then, will help him with his sense of direction.

Even more exact is the use of a compass, a little gadget that can actually tell a human which way is north. A little arrow in a box points in that direction no matter which way he holds it. With a compass it is very hard for the hunter to get lost, unless he forgets to bring it on the trip or leaves it back at camp.

A clever hunter is one who takes note of his surroundings with as many visual references as possible to help keep him oriented. Most hunting areas have several visual references. Windmills are common, and in some places, drilling derricks are also easily seen. There are overhead wires, pipelines, and, of course, fence lines that can also keep the hunter oriented. Following roads, fence lines, or other man-made references should keep the hunter out of trouble. I know not many hunters perish in the field, although some of them do require a search party. When this happens, the lost hunter usually has to face a great deal of criticism from the rest of the hunters in his group.

I think I better mention one other trick that prevents getting lost. It is just a way for the hunter to remember where he was, in case he wants to return to the same place. It is also a way for someone else to follow him when he is wandering about, usually on the trail of a wounded animal.

The scenario is something like this. A hunter shoots some game and the animal runs off. The hunter decides to find the game and starts tracking. It may take some time and cover a significant distance. The hunter may eventually find the game and by then has become so disoriented that he cannot find his way back to where he started. The answer to this problem is simple. The hunter should remember to mark the trail as he goes along. A smart hunter will provide himself with something to leave behind, at frequent points along the path he is taking, that will serve this purpose. This reminds me of the old fairy tale you used to tell me about Hansel and Gretel when they were wandering in the forest, except the smart hunter will not use bits of bread. Perhaps some paper tissue so commonly found in human dens would do, or perhaps small pieces of colored cloth or ribbon. There are many ways to mark a trail but the results are the same. The hunter will be able to find his way back or other hunters will be able to find him.

Take care of yourself, Dad.

Love,

Buck

Snake Bite—Bite Back

Deer Dad:

Are you taking care of yourself? I hope so; you're not getting any younger. Take your vitamins. Don't I sound like a parent? I wonder how many children I have?

Do you know what's nice about being a deer? It's really good to live in the country. Everything has its place. We know just where we belong. Mother Nature has taken care of us pretty well. Our biggest problem is the human, and, otherwise, we have little to fear.

Humans, on the other hand, don't do very well in the country. They have things to fear. There are many little critters that can really hurt them, even though the critters are much smaller than the human beings themselves. Why, even a little spider can make them very sick, or even do them in. Then, there are fire ants. Humans seem to have the unerring ability to find fire ants' homes and get themselves covered with these little devils.

That brings us to snakes. Humans think every snake is a bad snake. If they see a snake, they will try to kill it. They don't understand the important place snakes have in the ecological balance and how they eat rodents and other small animals so that we are not overrun. In fact, every animal in the world is really important and has a place in the order of things, and it's only when humans start to rearrange this order that they get into trouble.

Anyway, there are some snakes that are poisonous and can literally kill a human that gets in their way. So, humans should have a great deal of respect for these reptiles and learn how to deal with them if they intend to spend any time in the country.

First of all, an intelligent human will try to avoid encounters with snakes. He should know that snakes usually like dark places and prefer to stay in caves or holes. They also become quite dormant and slow moving in cold weather. In warm weather they like to come out and sun themselves. Hunters should try to stay out of caves and should not put their hands into holes and other places unless they know there is nothing in them. By the way, that

149

suggestion includes sleeping bags, boots, and all of the other things hunters use in the field.

Second, a human who is roaming about the countryside should wear appropriate protection in case a snake should attack. The best protection in this case is a pair of sturdy leather boots, preferably boots that have high tops, even to just below the knee. Then, if a snake does bite, the tough leather will protect the hunter's lower legs. Of course, these boots are expensive, but so are a good pair of legs.

What should the hunter do if he or a friend is bitten? Well, there are snake bite kits available that are small, compact, and will fit easily into some spare corner or pocket. The problem is the kits don't work well. If bitten, the hunter should wash the area of the bite thoroughly with soap and water. The bitten area (ie. arm or leg) should be splinted, and the human should be taken to the nearest emergency facility. Applying tourniquets or ice can do more harm than good.

The hunter must remember that just because a snake has bitten him, it does not mean that a lethal dose of venom has been injected. The amount of venom injected depends upon many factors including the quality of the bite and the depth of penetration as well as the amount of venom injected, which depends upon when the snake bit something last. Humans probably die more often from the shock of being bitten than the bite itself.

Nevertheless, if bitten by a snake that he suspects is poisonous, the hunter should seek medical attention quickly. It is very helpful to the doctor if the snake is brought along for accurate identification. There are very good methods of treating snake bites if treatment is begun and is specific. It is probably better to bring a dead snake into the office than a live one. Live snakes have never been popular with doctors or their office staffs.

Snake bites are not common, but just about every human has a deathly fear of snakes, and everyone knows one friend who has had serious trouble with one. Humans should just remember that the snake is far more afraid of the human than the human is of the snake. The snake would much rather not get involved and only does so when he has no other choice and is directly threatened.

I'm not even a deer doctor, much less a human one so, I had better end this letter now. Please don't forget about the vitamins.

Love,

Buck

That's a Funny Looking Deer

Deer Dad:

I saw that antelope the other day and he told me you had a cold, I hope you are over it by now. Speaking of antelopes, I thought I would mention that we deer are not the only "game in town," or at least in the country. Other wildlife are present in abundance and are worthy of mention since some of them are our friends. Now, of course, you realize that different parts of the country will have different species of game, and what's true in New York (wherever that is) will not be true in south Texas. Since we live in south Texas, I will confine my remarks to that geography. I hope New Yorkers will be tolerant.

First of all, there are naturally-occurring species and then there are the species of animals that humans have introduced artificially. You know, Dad, humans have been fooling around with manipulating our environment, and it's flora and fauna ever since they were able to walk and think. After many centuries, this has certainly impacted on us. I think all species, except perhaps the cockroach, have been affected. Things were bad enough when all humans had were clubs and spears but now with all their sophisticated equipment they can manipulate the environment to their heart's content. Well, several decades ago they thought they would just introduce animals from different parts of the world into our part. Some of these transplants failed easily, but some succeeded miserably.

To mention a few of the naturally occurring species that interest humans from a hunting point of view, I should first discuss the antelope, since he started this letter. Actually, the antelope falls into both the native and foreign categories of game. The Pronghorn antelope is a native American. In fact, it is the only one of the species native to this country. I'll talk about other antelopes later in the letter. The Pronghorn antelope is a beautiful animal, and, while both males and females have horns, the males' horns are quite large and distinctive. I have heard that their meat is quite tasty as well.

151

The other common game animals in my area are not as tasty, but they are popular among hunters. The coyote is actually quite hated by most landowners. This is true for a variety of reasons. Most landowners are sure that coyote attack young animals for food and, therefore, should be destroyed and eliminated from the range. Some areas actually have a bounty on coyote, they are so detested by humans. The sign of a true deer hunter is one who is able to avoid shooting at coyote lest the deer be scared away by the noise.

Javelina, officially called the collared peccary, is a rather fierce and ugly "pig like" looking animal, but not in the same family as swine, although this fact is not recognized by most hunters. They are quite funny looking as they scuttle about; they make impressive trophies when mounted with their mouths opened and their tusks bared in a snarl. I don't think humans like to eat javelina, although some say the babies' meat is quite tender.

Then there are wildcats. Wildcats are sought after by hunters as a trophy. They are wily, cunning, and difficult to shoot. Wildcats are usually mounted with their full body included, so the skin should be saved. They are impressively displayed in this manner.

Humans introduced foreign animals into this country from time to time in attempts to improve hunting excitement. Various species of deer from foreign lands, such as the Sika deer from Japan, the Fallow deer from Europe, and the Axis deer from Asia have not gained widespread status. Although they are quite rare in most parts of the country, these animals do appear from time to time and thoroughly confuse the novice hunter.

Several varieties of wild sheep have also been introduced. In my part of the country the most popular variety is the Aoudad. Originally found in Africa, this very strong and hearty species can and usually does take over the range and forces other game out of the area. Aoudad run in herds and are difficult to track, shoot, and kill. Hunters often feel that bullets simply bounce off them. Considerable skill is required to get a trophy but they make a beautiful mount. Mouflon sheep, originally from Corsica and Sardinia, have also been transplanted into this country. The meat of these wild sheep, I have heard, is often tough and not very tasty.

That brings me to the black buck antelope, originally found in India. Beautiful animals with long spiral horns, they run and leap very fast and high when challenged. The meat of these animals is reported to be very tasty.

Another common animal found in various parts of the country is the feral hog. These hogs were originally domesticated but then allowed to run wild. They are said to be good to eat and also difficult to kill. They, too, make interesting and fierce trophies.

Of course, Dad, other species of animals are found in hunting areas. Some ranchers are fond of keeping pets such as buffalo, camels, and domesticated animals such as goats, sheep, cows, children, and in-laws. Some deer are also treated as pets by the landowner. These may have special collars or ear tags to identify them. It would not be considered good taste to destroy one of the landowner's favorite pets.

Send my regards to all our friends. I will write again soon.

Love,

Buck

My Friend the Cop

Deer Dad:

I could hardly wait until I had time to write. I want to tell you what happened to me today. I don't remember if I ever told you about the game warden who patrols my area. He really is a wonderful human who looks out for the welfare of all the animals under his jurisdiction. Today was an example of just how important game wardens are to our survival.

During the past several weeks a series of poachers have been sneaking onto the ranch where I live. They come in at night to hunt. They even use a spotlight to find us in the dark. I don't really understand my fascination with spotlights. Every deer I have spoken to seems to have the same reaction. We see the light, look directly at it, and thereby give ourselves away to the illegal and dangerous night hunter. It has something to do with the fact that our pupils are dilated at night. We have a special reflective surface behind our retina that glows when a light is flashed on it. Anyway, it's a dead giveaway, and I do mean dead.

Well, the rancher that owns our property is pretty fussy about who he lets hunt here and is very protective of his ranch. He has been trying to catch these poachers for some time and frequently stays up nights driving around the ranch. There is a highway on one edge of the property and poachers can all too easily sneak in and out undetected. Last night the rancher and game warden got together and, by staying hidden and communicating with two-way radios, were able to find and apprehend the criminals. It was quite a sight watching those two poachers trying to explain why they were on the property with spotlights and rifles. The game warden took their weapons and issued them citations. The trouble is I'm not sure they will really pay much of a penalty for their crime. They may be found guilty, pay a fine, and get a probated sentence. I just wish the judges recognized the serious nature of the offense and punished these humans in a fair manner. You know, I can read normal human books. I just wish I could understand the words in those law books I found. I would take those poachers to court myself. From what I know about the legal system in this country, it wouldn't be too absurd to see a deer in court. One sees just about everything else.

At any rate, the danger is over for now. I'm sure there will be more poachers before long since it is well known that our ranch has some of the best deer in the country. I just hope our game warden stays alert and remains as friendly to us as he has been in the past.

Take care of yourself. It's getting colder, and the rut will soon be upon us again. Please remember your age and try not to get too excited. I'd much prefer you sit back and reminisce about the old days rather then go out and show off beyond your abilities. I don't want to be an orphan just yet.

Love,

Buck

It's Against the Law

Deer Dad:

I have written to you about out of season and night hunting. They are clearly illegal. Unfortunately, those are not the only illegal activities that humans like to perpetrate against the landowner and the game. There are many others, all designed by unscrupulous humans to take what is plainly not theirs.

There are two problems with these activities. First of all, stealing other human's property is not good. Secondly, during the act of stealing this property the thief (also called poacher) usually displays little regard for the rest of the landowner's property and will usually cut fences and leave gates open, potentially causing much more damage than just the loss of a deer (although I can't think of anything worse).

The methods used by these poachers is, at times, truly ingenious. Once they find a good base of operations on someone else's property, they may actually set up camp and stay for several days. If they perceive little risk because of infrequent or absent inspections by the landowner or his employees, they may develop large scale operations, literally raping the entire property of its valuable game.

Other poachers specialize in lightening raids into and out of a property rapidly to avoid detection. Some hunt what has become known as "the long narrow pasture," driving along roads looking for deer just inside the fence lines, stopping just long enough to kill the deer and remove him, then go on their way again. It's amazing how they may do this even on well traveled highways, during the day or night, climbing over a high fence or going through it, with little regard for passing motorists or other human observation.

I mentioned the use of helicopters when taking deer surveys. I also mentioned their use in illegal deer hunting. Helicopters can be used effectively to chase deer, often to exhaustion, and corral us into small areas where we can be easily harvested. As you know, Dad, it is very difficult for a deer to remain hidden with the threat of a helicopter overhead. The noise and wind created by these infernal machines usually scares us half to death and the tendency is to get up and run. Actually, the best advice I can give to any young and inexperienced deer is to try to remain hidden whenever danger seems imminent. Generally, it has always worked to my advantage to stay put. The danger will usually pass and a good, well chosen hiding place will serve over and over again.

Remember, Dad, our biggest allies in all these illegal activities are the game wardens. They are our only true friends. The wardens will protect us to the fullest extent of the law. These poorly paid, hard working individuals are uniformly imbued with a sense of justice that makes them indispensable to our survival as a species. Without them, we would be wiped out in a few years. Most other humans have little sense of integrity when it comes to choosing between sound ecological practices to preserve the flora and fauna of our world and the selfish destruction of anything they perceive to be to their immediate and short term advantage. Many humans are rather shortsighted in this regard and do not truly see the relationship of their own frail existence to the overall evolution of our world. Oops, this is beginning to sound like a sermon.

I guess it's not too bad for us. Look how humans are trying to eliminate the cockroach. Interestingly enough, they are failing. Both the cockroach and the deer were around before humans crawled out of the sea, and I hope we will be here long after. I know the cockroach will succeed. They don't grow large racks of antlers. They also taste lousy. We, on the other hand, need all the help we can get. The game wardens help us and for this we should be eternally grateful. I just wish there was some tangible way we could reward them. One day we may be able to afford a lobby effort in the state capitol to convince our legislators to remunerate the wardens appropriately. Until then, they can certainly share whatever I have, anytime.

Talking about all this illegal stuff really makes me depressed. I am going to end this letter and go out and get a nice drink (of water) and eat some acorns. Take care of yourself.

Love,

Buck

Rules, Rules, Rules

Deer Dad:

I know you have been around a long time. One of the reasons we both are still here is that we have learned the rules of survival. We know where it is secure to go and not to go. We know when it is hazardous to go and not to go. We have learned through experience and with some luck that certain activities will be safe and others, not.

Another reason we have survived is because hunters have rules they have to follow when hunting. Actually, hunters have rules they have to follow for almost everything they want to do. They call these rules laws. Laws govern almost every human activity. For example, they regulate who drives a vehicle. They prohibit many human activities, such as stealing, murder, and something called rape. They regulate individuals, groups, nations, and, best of all, hunters.

I already described our friends, the game wardens, in regard to poachers. Well, the game wardens enforce a variety of other laws about hunting that even the odds a bit for us. Humans call it "sporting." Really, it just gives us the edge we need to keep ahead of them.

For example, hunters can't hunt twenty four hours a day. In fact, hunting at night is highly illegal. As you know, it's done all too often, mainly because there are just too few game wardens to keep everyone honest.

It's also illegal to hunt from helicopters, to use dogs (in most states), and to kill too many of us.

There are also some rules that are not laws. Rules that are not laws often vary from place to place and from landowner to landowner. For example, there are some landowners who refuse to use feeders as a way to attract us. They believe feeders give the hunter an unfair edge in the sport. Deer feeders are quite commonly used by some hunters in an attempt to artificially increase the odds of success in their favor. Many of the less intelligent or experienced of our species will disregard all the warning signals and frequent deer feeders in an attempt to get a "lazy deer's meal." Such a practice will often result

159

in an easy kill for the hunter. The deer become so used to eating at the feeder and so lazy eating at other times that all the hunter has to do is hang around the feeder and wait. Fortunately, the best deer are also the most intelligent and won't fall for that trick. I guess that's why we are the best. We have no intention of committing suicide.

When a hunter first starts to hunt on a property he had better find out what the "house" rules are that have been set down by his host or landowner. Sometimes they will include shooting only one sex or a limited number of deer. Sometimes they will be to not shoot some particular animal, often specially marked. A smart hunter will not commit some unauthorized act and thereby incur the disfavor of his host. It could easily signal the end of the relationship.

A rule of major importance is that there is a hunting season and that we are not at risk all year long. The season varies from place to place but is always in the fall and early winter after our racks have grown and we have become the best trophies. I guess most hunters wouldn't be very interested in us if the season occurred after we had shed our antlers. It would be a good trick to play on them if we could rearrange our physiology and shed our antlers just at the start of the season.

Well, Dad, maybe someday we can gain the advantage, meanwhile be careful and follow our own rules.

Love,

Buck

Which One is Mine?

Deer Dad:

I hope this letter finds you well. In fact, I hope this letter finds you at all. I'm never sure when I write to you that the postdeer (what did you expect—postman) will locate you. I know you are where you always are, but I can't be sure the postal service is accurate. Humans have these things called zip codes, but I understand even humans occasionally mess up mail delivery.

I am not writing to talk to you about the mail service. I am writing to tell you a story I heard about some hunters that was just too strange to be anything other than true. It seems one of them shot a rather scrawny deer one morning while his "buddy," hunting in the next pasture, shot a fine buck with a good rack. They field dressed their respective deer and brought them back to camp just about the same time. They hung them up, washed them out, and went inside to clean up. What they didn't do in the field and, even worse, what they didn't do at camp, was to tag their deer.

Now, Dad, remember I told you about rules humans have. They must obey these rules or law enforcement humans will get very angry at them and either arrest them or give them a citation which will cost them money. Well, one of the most important rules is that every hunter has to buy a license in order to hunt. This license gives the hunter permission to hunt in any particular state but also limits the hunter as to the kind and number of animals he is allowed to shoot.

Even though there are many deer, there are even more hunters. Hunters can shoot only a few deer each, otherwise I'm sure you realize that the world would rapidly run out of deer. Not a pleasant thought. Not only that, the sex of the deer shot is important and is regulated by the state officials.

When a hunter purchases a license, in addition to the main part of the document there are smaller sections that are called "tags." Tags are meant to be separated from the license and attached to the deer. They identify the deer as belonging to the owner of the license. When the hunter uses all of his tags, he has to stop hunting.

161

Now, to get back to the story. After the hunters cleaned up, one went inside to take a nap and the other went outside to tag his deer. He looked at both animals and realized that his deer didn't compare to the fine specimen that his friend had shot. Remembering that blood is thicker than water and venison is tastier than friendship, he immediately removed a tag from his license and affixed it to the antlers of his friend's deer—perhaps I should say his ex-friend.

The hunter knew that what he did was morally and probably legally wrong. He also realized that he could make many friends but would probably not find a trophy like this for many years. After he tagged the deer, his "ex friend" could do precious little about correcting the situation.

I know this story sounds far-fetched, but I ask you to recall some of the things you have seen hunters do during the years you have been hunter watching. Such a story is not impossible.

Take care of yourself. I will write again soon and hope the mail service will deliver the letter.

Love,

Buck

A Bad Disease

Deer Dad:

I couldn't wait to get home to tell you what I saw today. It was a classic case. The diagnosis was easy and I had a load of fun observing the symptoms. The diagnosis, deer Dad, was "buck fever," and a very advanced case I don't mind telling you.

I got up early today; it was well before sunrise. I was wandering about when I heard a pickup truck approaching. My usual tendency is to move away from such sounds, especially during hunting season, for obvious reasons. Today, for some unknown reason, I just decided to follow the truck.

As the truck passed rather close to where I was standing I knew that I had made the right choice. Sitting in the passenger seat was a hunter, or at least a human who was trying to be a hunter. He was obviously a brand new hunter. He had brand new hunting clothes (and the wrong kind, but I have written you about the right kind). He had a brand new rifle in his hands, which he didn't even know how to hold, and he had that look on his face that clearly demonstrated a combination of expectancy and fear.

I followed the truck, from a safe distance, to the blind where the driver deposited the hunter and left him to his own devices. Well, almost left him. He did make sure the hunter got into the blind. That wasn't very easy since he had to climb three steps and crawl through a hole in the floor. The hunter was rather portly and it took a bit of huffing and puffing to get through the hole. Then the truck drove away.

The hunter eventually managed to sit down, open up the windows on all four sides, get out all of his equipment, and arrange everything as he thought appropriate and then take stock of his surroundings. By this time it was just starting to get light, so I could see everything very well. Unfortunately for the new hunter, he could not. He kept swiveling around searching for some sign of deer. I guess I fooled him by standing right in the middle of the open space artificially created by the landowner. I will admit that I did stay downwind, so that I could smell the hunter (not that he could ever smell me). I decided that this would be a good experiment. I knew that he was instructed to keep his eyes on the edges of the brush where I might come out. He never did look in the middle.

He did make a good deal of noise as he was doing all of this arranging and looking. Any self respecting animal would never have come anywhere close to the blind under normal circumstances. The hunter also kept looking the wrong way. He was looking where there was most light. That also was upwind from me. When he did glance downwind he was so out of position that it would have taken five minutes for him to get ready to take a shot. I felt very safe.

Well, the sun was coming up pretty well by then. I knew no other game was in the area and this hunter was not going to have much of a story to tell unless I took the initiative. I purposely made some noise and he turned my way. It took a while for him to see me and even longer for him to get into an appropriate shooting position. I was prepared to run away before he was ready when I heard a shot ring out. It appeared to come from behind the blind but it certainly wasn't in my direction. It only took me a moment to realize that my hunter had gotten so excited that he accidently shot a hole in the roof of the blind. I realized I had absolutely nothing to worry about so I stayed put.

The crazy fool took two more shots, neither one in my direction. It was almost as if he purposely tried to miss me. One shot came dangerously close to a cow that happened to meander close to the blind. The other hit the dirt closer to the blind than to me. The wild look in the hunter's eye clearly indicated his panic and confusion. I wanted to reach out and offer help, but instead I decided that discretion was the better part of valor, so I left.

I didn't go far, however. I decided to stay around and see what happened when my hunter got picked up later in the morning. Sure enough, his driver asked him what he had seen. He replied nothing at all. He claimed only to have heard some shots nearby, saying they sounded like they were from hunters on the next property across the highway.

The driver was the son of the landowner. He knew the property well and we had seen each other several times. He had sort of a smirk on his face as he commiserated with the hunter and assured him he would have better luck that evening. Just as the driver bent down to pick up a spent shell casing, I snorted. I'm sure he heard me from the expression on his face, and I know we both had a good laugh about it. I hope he will tell his friends, just as I am telling you. It's really a good story.

Take care of yourself, especially during the hunting season, and please don't try to do what I did. It can be dangerous.

Love,

Buck

Tall Tales

Deer Dad:

As you know, hunting season lasts only a few months. What about the rest of the year? The rest of the year hunters should be preparing for next season. There is really so much to do I don't see how a hunter could even do any human type work. Instead, all of his time should be spent preparing. After all, that's all we deer do. We get ready for next year. Humans, however, have other priorities during the "off season."

First of all, they have to work. That's so they can get enough money to pay for their hunting costs, which by now even you, Dad, realize are rather expensive. They also have a variety of leisure activities that consume inordinate amounts of time and detract from the important goal of hunting preparation.

Many hunters have wives. Wives are an interesting group. They need attention and money. They thoroughly confuse the hunter. I really can't imagine how just one wife can do all that damage. After all, we don't have any trouble from the females of our species. They pretty much leave us alone except during the rut. Even then they don't get very possessive and, in fact, don't seem to mind which male mates with them. Certainly they have no interest in us the rest of the year and we get along quite well.

The humans have a different story. Their wives are very possessive. If a human male so much as looks at another female, he is in plenty of trouble. If he does more than just look, he risks great difficulty which could end up in his losing hunting time or, worse, losing hunting privileges on the wife's property.

Then, there are children. Both humans and deer have children. Children are very important to the survival of the species, but, deer children and human children are certainly treated differently. Our children spend one or two years with their mothers, learn about life, and then go about their way. Human children spend years and years with their parents and actually never leave home. Oh, they may move out of the den and eventually find a wife and raise their own children, but they continue to remain members of the "family," and the relationship never ends. That has both advantages and disadvantages.

For humans, family is nice to have when you get old and need someone to take care of you, but other times families can be quite difficult. Dealing with teenagers, for example, can be a very trying on the nerves. Human parents think that when one of their children is in his "terrible two's" life gets pretty difficult, but then the children get older and things get worse and worse. There is a time, usually during the child's twenties, when the family relationship becomes tolerable, but, believe me, it's not worth much during the teenage years.

So there's work, wives, and children to name just a few distractions for the hunters. To make matters worse, what little time he does have to prepare for next season he spends incorrectly. He doesn't worry about things like caring for his weapons, scouting the property, and other important activities. Instead, he spends his time thinking up tall tales and jokes to share with his hunting "buddies" during next hunting season.

Let me tell you Dad, each year the tales get taller and taller. I could fill books with them, but I haven't got the space. Also, most of them are so silly that I haven't got the patience. Many of the stories relate to past glories. Hunting stories are only some of the tall tales told. There are college stories, employer stories, and women stories. They don't sound very funny to me, but they really make the humans laugh. Sometimes only half of them laugh, other times the other half. That usually happens when the story is about one or another group of them.

Better their time should be spent in serious preparation for the next season. Oh well, I guess they never learn. Take care of yourself. I'll write again soon.

Love,

Buck

Excuses, Excuses

Deer Dad:

You know, Dad, after a while you hear just about everything. After a few hunting seasons listening to these human hunters, I have heard just about every possible excuse for lack of success. Of course, lack of success means different things to different humans. Lack of success may mean not getting a shot at a deer, shooting and missing, shooting the "wrong" deer, shooting too few or too many deer, shooting a cow instead of a deer, or anything else imaginable.

I have been keeping track of some of the excuses I have heard. Since it's rather sunny today and really good hunting weather, I thought I'd stay bedded down in some heavy brush and write you some of the excuses hunters use.

These excuses fall into categories.
1. No Shot:
   • A tree (bush, branch, etc.) was in the way.
   • He moved at the last minute.
   • My rifle jammed.
   • He wasn't big enough.
   • It was too dark.
   • It was a buck and I wanted a doe (and vice versa).
   • I just like to look.
2. Missed Shot:
   • I'm sure I hit him. He must be injured.
   • That tree moved in the way.
   • A fly landed on my sight and must have moved it.
   • He jumped just as I shot.
   • I blinked.
   • I was aiming at a different deer.
3. Wrong Shot:
   • It sure looked like a deer to me.
   • It moved.
   • It looked bigger in my telescopic sight.
   • I just wanted some meat.

Well, Dad there are many many more. I just didn't want to bore you with too many. I know as you get older your attention span decreases. It happens to all of us. I even hear tell it happens to humans. They even have a name for the disease that causes older humans to lose their memory, but I can't remember what they call it. Anyway, for all the excuses there is only one statement that really matters when the hunter gets less than he bargained for during a hunt. About all he can say is that he messed up and that he learned from his mistake. The truth is the best explanation.

I've written to you about the large jar some landowners keep in camp into which hunters place a predetermined amount of money when they shoot and don't bring in any meat. These jars usually fill up nicely by the end of the season (thank God).

Love,

Buck

Ho Ho

Deer Dad:

As you know, humans are funny people. Hunters are very funny people. Funny can be defined many ways and most all definitions apply to hunters. They are funny-strange. They are also funny-funny. They love to play jokes on one another. Sometimes these jokes are simple stories they tell about each other. Sometimes the jokes are quite elaborate events contrived to fool each other. I would like to tell you about one joke that illustrates my point.

Let me set the scene for you. The hunting season is drawing to a close. One hunter has yet to see, much less kill, a decent buck all season. The weather is getting bad for the hunter (good for the deer), since there is a large amount of fog each morning and evening. The hunter is getting desperate and the comments from his "friends" are getting more caustic as the end of the season draws near.

One day, while driving around the ranch with some of his "buddies," all of whom have semi-trophy deer in the cooler, he sits in the bed of the pickup truck searching until his eyes are ready to fall out of his head. Suddenly, the driver slams on the brakes and points toward some trees about one hundred and fifty yards ahead. Hidden in the trees with some of his head and body showing is a beautiful fourteen point buck with a mighty rack and a huge body. The buck is standing sideways looking directly at the truck. The hunter sees the deer and has a fairly good shot if he chooses to take it.

Emotions and adrenaline take over. In a split second the hunter's thoughts race through his entire hunting life. Never has he seen such an animal as this. Never this late in the season has he failed to get a buck and never have his friends in the truck urged him so forcefully to take a shot.

He takes as careful an aim as possible, considering all the pressure on him to do well. When the smoke clears, the deer is still there, and he obviously missed completely. He has heard stories that a wild shot will often not startle the deer (Have you ever heard such a crazy idea?), so he prepares to shoot again. Again, his friends urge him on.

171

Again, he misses. Another shot, why not? And another! And another!

It takes four or five shots before the hunter realizes what has happened. What has happened, of course, is that there is no deer there at all, or, at least, not a live one.

Now, Dad, can you imagine anybody going to the trouble of making a full mount of a trophy whitetail deer just so that he could fool his friends into taking shot after shot in a desperate attempt to satisfy some primitive hunting urge? Well, I've seen it happen. Then, after the joke is over, everybody laughs and laughs and all the red-faced hunter can do is make some lame excuse and shrug it off. Of course, he does have one other option and that's to figure some way to play some other type of joke on those who played this one on him.

I thought you would get a kick out of that story. I hope I was right.

Love,

Buck

Happy News

Deer Dad:

Today I have a surprise for you. My son, your grandson, has written his first letter. I received it in the mail, and I thought you would like to read it. I am quite proud of his abilities, although I'm not sure of his sanity.

Love,

Buck

From My Son

Deer Dad:

Hey, baby! How are the wife and kids? I want to tell you about something that happened to me recently. I was walking through the park one day, just walking through the park, when all of a sudden a strange antelope came out and started whispering strange nothings in my ear. Well, needless to say I was completely confused, so I took off at a trot. The antelope followed me and finally overtook me at the Washburn's old rusty water tower, bolted around me, and cut me off. Then she opened her mouth and asked me if I wanted anything to eat. I asked her what her wares were, and she said (among other things) melons. I then proceeded to ask her how much she wanted for the melons and if they were ripe. Before I could finish my question, she screamed out (obscenities omitted), "How dare you question an antelope's cantaloupes!!!"

Well, see you soon and love to the family.

Buck Jr.

Want Advice? Don't Ask Ann Landers

Deer Dad:

We're having some rain. It sure feels good after all the dry weather. My part of the country never seems to get enough rain and you know that makes for a hard winter. I have to keep going down to a small creek pretty far from home and I just don't like it.

I was watching some humans the other day. One of them had what was obviously a new rifle. He was trying to figure out how to work it. I could tell he really didn't understand and even with failure after failure the one thing he didn't ever do was get help. Humans are funny about that and hunters are especially funny. They just don't like to admit to each other that there may be something they don't know. What's worse, there was a book of instructions nearby, but the hunter simply refused to read them.

A smart hunter will be smart enough to get help when he needs it. Unfortunately, there doesn't seem to be many smart hunters. There are plenty of sources for help and many individuals who would be more than happy to give advice if asked. I will admit that some of these humans who just love to give advice to others don't know much themselves and certainly are not experts. So, the hunter looking for help had better make sure that his "expert" really is an expert.

There are true experts available. Some of them give lectures for which other humans pay money to hear. Many of these people really do know what they are talking about and have proven to other humans that their advice is good. New hunters should attend these lectures, especially those about gun safety.

Other sources can even be personal friends and other hunters. Once again, however, it's nice to know the credentials of the person giving advice to be sure the advice is accurate and knowledgeable.

Even if there is no live person to give advice, humans can watch video tapes prepared by experts. These tapes are played on television sets, and television sets seem to be everywhere in the human world.

Humans are always watching them anyway, so they might as well use them for some good purpose such as hunting education.

Then there are books. There are books and books and books. Everyone seems to be interested in writing books. Some of them are quite good and authoritative; others are fairly worthless. There are groups of humans called "critics" who tell other humans which books are good and which are not. Critics are usually knowledgeable but are always very important to authors who want their books accepted. The hunter truly interested in educating himself will acquire several hunting books geared to his particular interest and study these books carefully.

There are also newspapers and magazines. Some of them are general publications that contain hunting sections, and others are devoted entirely to the various aspects of hunting. Most of them have pictures as well, and they are usually quite instructive.

Some of the best publications are produced and distributed by the Parks and Wildlife Departments of the various states in which hunting is permitted. These publications are written by true experts, deemed so not only due to their education, but also because of their practical experience. I have seen some of these publications and they are indeed factual and accurate. Often they are free, which should make them very popular with the hunter; however, even if they do cost some money they are well worth the investment.

Finally, the hunter that really wants a first-hand education and on the spot training could hire a guide to accompany him on the hunting trip and teach him exactly what to do when. Guides are expensive, but good ones are certainly worth their fees.

Clearly, Dad, the hunter that thinks he doesn't need help at all is really making a mistake and asking for trouble. Enough about education for now. I have to go find a good book for myself. I think I'll just curl up with a good novel until the rain stops.

Love,

Buck

The Bottom Line—Flexibility

Deer Dad:

The more time I spend watching humans, the stranger they seem. I was passing by the camp house on my ranch the other day when I saw the strangest thing I have ever seen. Three hunters were standing outside the house shooting pistols at a tin can. The can was probably 50 yards from them and they were all aiming very carefully and shooting as fast as they could pull the trigger. Needless to say, none of them hit the can with any of the shots. Boy, did they waste bullets, and the noise they were making would have raised the dead. They seemed to be having the greatest time so I thought I would give them a real thrill. I ran within a hundred yards from them just about the time I calculated their pistols would be empty. They went crazy. Of course, it wouldn't have mattered if their pistols were full, they couldn't have hit me anyway. I have seen hunters actually use pistols to hunt deer. They had deluded themselves into thinking they were great shots. I'd show myself to them time after time with complete safety. They might as well have hunted with a camera for all the trophies they got.

Anyway, Dad, that's not why I am writing this letter. Instead, I want to discuss one trait that hunters should have but rarely do. That is flexibility. A successful hunter must be flexible in his plans and activities. The more flexibility he has, the more likely he is to repeat past successes. He must remember there is always another way to do something.

Flexibility is enhanced by preparation. If the hunter prepares for only one eventuality, then he loses his options. If he prepares for every eventuality he can imagine, then he can be truly flexible.

Therefore, the smart hunter knows that he must be ready for both heavy rain and desert type dryness during the same trip. He must prepare for intense heat and frigid cold in the same day. Insects, snakes, cacti, barbed wire, and any other imaginable sharp object will sting, bite, or impale him with regularity. There will be clear weather until he sees some game and then fog will immediately set in, and it goes on and on. He is guaranteed to experience the unexpected unless he expects it.

The smart hunter should be prepared to adopt alternate hunting techniques when the ones he is using do not work. He must be able to hunt from a blind, from a vehicle, or on foot at different times of day and under different conditions. If he knows all the usual ways to hunt, he must also be ready to develop some new and innovative methods on the spot. Then, he just might begin to understand the vagaries of the sport. Before that he can expect frustration after frustration. Only the most tenacious will continue. That's good for us. Most humans lose interest after awhile. Our biggest threat is a neophyte hunter who succeeds on his first experience. He will then think he can repeat this at will and we will be stuck with another bumbling but avid hunter.

I heard another example of beginners luck the other day. Humans have a place called Las Vegas where they go to throw away their money in an indoor sport they call "gambling." If they win the first time there, the humans will return time after time to try to repeat the process. They are usually unsuccessful. I know of one human who understands the problem very well and doesn't bother to go to Las Vegas any more. He just mails them a check once a year. He avoids a common human problem called ulcers.

Enough about flexibility. One of the ways to demonstrate flexibility is to know when to quit. I will write again soon.

Love,

Buck

When to Stop Hunting

Deer Dad:

I heard an interesting discussion the other day which gave me cause to think. I'd like to share it with you, Dad, because it really is quite important.

Two hunters were talking about a third and were concerned that their friend was getting quite old, probably too old to hunt. They were discussing when to stop hunting. I began thinking about the best answer to that discussion. Of course, it all depends upon who you are asking, as to the correct answer. If you are a deer, you would probably say the best time for a human to stop hunting is at birth.

There are times when the hunter must obviously stop hunting. At night and at the end of the season are two times that come to mind immediately. After that, from the hunter's point of view, there is probably no time that is correct to stop except for death.

By the way, Dad, I'm sure you realize that even humans leave this earth some day. In fact, the average life span of a human is probably around seventy five years and many of them hunt right up to the end.

As a human gets older, it becomes more and more difficult for him to get out into the field and hunt. Believe me, I have seen some strange sights during even my few years on this earth when it comes to the accommodations humans will make to continue to hunt. Whatever their physical status or impairment, they usually can find a way to fulfill their primitive urges.

One day I saw a group of humans carry a very old man into a ground blind at the edge of an oat field, position him just right, literally aim his rifle to the middle of the field, place it in the hunter's hands and drive away. A few hours later, I'll be darned if he didn't shoot a nice buck that inadvertently walked into the field not realizing the hunter was there. Later, when his friends returned, they had to describe the configuration of the deer to the hunter who wasn't even sure when or how he shot the deer.

I have seen hunters so obese that they literally had to be hoisted into a raised box blind because they couldn't climb the ladder by themselves. I have seen visually impaired hunters, hunters missing one or both legs who hunted from wheelchairs, hunters with only one arm, and hunters with a variety of other disabilities that would have made a hospital administrator's pulse quicken at the thought of having such a human in their institution.

There is such a thing as common sense, and common sense has to be coupled with safety—safety for the hunter and safety for other hunters in the area. It doesn't make any sense at all to hasten a human's demise through unnecessary exertion chasing after deer or other game over rough country. Then again, Dad, we know that these hunters are strange beings and there is no accounting for their actions. Just about the only thing we can count on is that we can't predict anything they might do.

Enough of this small talk. Take care of yourself and remember that no matter what the human looks like or how weak or disabled he might appear, he is always dangerous.

Love,

Buck

A Good Hunter

Deer Dad:

I have been thinking a great deal about hunters recently. You know, there are all kinds. Not only do they look different from each other, but they also act different. I'm not talking about the fact that some are old and some young, some thin and some fat, some rich and some poor. It's just that some are good people and some are bad. I never really had much trouble with good and bad before, but, when placing these labels on hunters, it does become important. Our survival, not only as individuals but also as a species, depends upon good hunters, and we are at risk with bad hunters. On the whole, the good outnumber the bad right now. I hope it stays that way. I think this subject is so important that I will try to define a good hunter. I will save the definition of a bad hunter for another letter.

First of all a good hunter practices safety measures. I cannot overemphasize the importance of safety. A good hunter is cautious for himself, other humans, animals, and plant life as well. Safety can be learned and it must be practiced. Prudent hunting practices are usually harder to maintain than careless ones, but they are of utmost importance. It actually takes work to be safe and a lazy hunter, therefore, is probably a dangerous one.

A good hunter is a considerate hunter. There are many things to be considerate about when hunting. It goes without saying that the hunter must be compassionate of the game and wildlife he encounters. He must be protective of the land and, of course, the landowner. This type of consideration has a selfish significance if the hunter wants to be invited back at a future time. He should also be aware of the domesticated animals in the area. They are important to the landowner as well, usually more important than the deer and other game. Of course, he must be good-natured with other hunters. Etiquette is essential when dealing with other humans.

A good hunter is a conservationist. He is aware of the natural resources in the area and ensures that he protects them at all times. He does nothing to diminish the value of the property on which he is hunting. I once heard a human teenager, a true conservationist, comment about this subject when she was about to leave on a camping trip. She said, "Take nothing but pictures, leave nothing but footprints."

A good hunter must be a student of the sport. He must recognize that there is always something new to learn about hunting, and he must be willing and even somewhat fanatical about learning as much as possible all the time. Not only must he become educated about hunting, but he must educate as well. He must pass on what he learns to others and endeavor to create an educational atmosphere wherever he goes.

A good hunter is humane. A humane human is not always easy to find. I would like to think that a charitable quality is present in all humans and that when they act otherwise it is out of emotion and not premeditation. Acting in a decent manner, especially to the victims of the hunt, is essential.

Finally, if these letters ever are to get published in book form, a good hunter is one who purchases this book—not only a good hunter but also a friend. I'll write soon about bad hunters.

Love,

Buck

A Bad Hunter

Deer Dad:

This may be the shortest letter I have ever written to you. I promised I would tell you the characteristics of a bad hunter. I have thought long and hard about it.

A bad hunter is a hunter who does everything opposite of the good hunter I described in my last letter. Enough said!

Love,

Buck

P.S. Oh yes, Dad, a bad hunter is also one who doesn't buy these letters when I publish them in a book.
B.

Hunting Buddies

Deer Dad:

Most humans are groupies. They have some sort of herd instinct, like sheep. They generally do not like to be alone. Although there are some exceptions, they really do much better when they are around others of their species, but not just with any members. They much prefer to associate with other humans who share the same interests. Although that is usually the case, the only exception appears to be when they take a mate. Then, for some strange reason, they usually pick someone with opposite interests. Of course, Dad, this leads to many interesting situations and misadventures and often ends in a strange rite called divorce which is just too complicated to describe. All I can tell you is I'm grateful we don't have either marriage or divorce. Our life is much simpler. From human activities I have observed, some humans feel the same as we do, moving from partner to partner with the same ease we enjoy.

Anyway, marriage aside, human groups usually share the same interests. Of course, humans can belong to many groups and often move from one to another just as easily as they change their clothes. At least, some can. Some humans move from place to place but never change their manner or style. Others move from place to place and group to group and have the ability to behave like a chameleon, adopting the style and habits of the group they are in at the time. That is why, I am told, so many cowboy clothes are sold in New York City.

Belonging to a group has many advantages for its members. If it's a group of humans in the same business, then they will benefit financially from their mutual efforts at working together. If it's a group of humans participating in the same sport, then a team effort will result in a win for the whole group.

When humans hunt together, they form bonds of friendship that usually last the test of time. Even if they associate with each other only during the period of the hunt just once a year, nevertheless they develop a commonalty of interests that allows them to resume a relationship during those infrequent meetings. Moreover, initial meetings at a hunt often blossom into close and lasting friendships, relationships that continue throughout the year even when hunting is not the binding force.

Much can be said for these "fringe benefits" of hunting. I, alone, can take credit for bringing many humans closer together. Friendships have been formed many times in a hunting lodge after sharing stories of my legendary traits.

To illustrate how hunting accomplishes true miracles in this regard, I need only remind you that hunting parties have produced lasting friendships between such diverse individuals as rich men and poor men, athletes and college professors, and even doctors and lawyers.

Yes, Dad, hunting buddies have gone a long way toward producing peace in the world, almost as much as Santa Claus and Mickey Mouse.

Please take care of yourself and keep away from all those hunting buddies.

Love,

Buck

Parting Words

Deer Dad:

I know I have not written to you in a while. For this, I apologize. I have been doing a great deal of thinking. I have come to a decision. As you remember, I have mentioned that I thought I might collect the letters I have written to you and actually publish them in a book.

Well, neither you nor I are getting any younger. In fact, I can certainly tell the years have taken their toll on me. I don't know how much longer I can survive the rigors of the fight for survival against nature and hunters, and I want to leave something lasting in this world.

I realize that publishing some of the letters I have written may compromise friends and relatives of ours. On the other hand, there is no question that if a hunter learns even a small amount from reading the book and develops an improved sense of game management and hunting technique, then we will be better off as a species. Oh, I'm not so naive as to think that these letters contain such words of wisdom that no one can manage without committing them to memory, but I do feel that they contain kernels of truth. They may even have value to both the experienced and novice hunter.

So, Dad, I'm going to do it. As a matter of fact, this will be my last letter to you because I want to get them and take all of them to the publisher. I know you have enjoyed these letters. I have enjoyed writing them. What I really want is for you to visit me and bring them with you. I am enclosing a map with directions to my ranch. We need to spend some time together before we run out of time.

Take care of yourself for now. I will send you a copy of the book when it is available. I will even sign it with my hoof.

Love,

Buck